The National Action Committee on the Status of Women's Voters' Guide

A Women's Agenda for Social Justice

Edited by Nandita Sharma

James Lorimer & Company, Publishers
Toronto, 1997

James Lorimer & Company Ltd. acknowledges with thanks the support of the Canada Council and the Ontario Arts Council in the development of writing and publishing in Canada.

Canadian Cataloguing in Publication Data

The National Action Committee on the Status of Women's voters' guide

ISBN 1-55028-552-1

1. Women - Government policy - Canada.
   2. Women - Social conditions - Canada.
   3. Political parties - Canada - Platforms.
   4. Canada - Politics and government - 1993–
   * I. Sharma, Nandita Rani, 1964 –. II. National Action Committee on the Status of Women. III. Title: Voters' guide.

HQ1236.5.C2N37 1997   305.4'0971   C97-930932-8

James Lorimer & Company Ltd., Publishers
35 Britain Street
Toronto, Ontario
M5A 1R7

Printed and bound in Canada

Table of Contents

Acknowledgements

The National Action Committee on the Status of Women's Voters' Guide: A Women's Agenda for Social Justice is a project of the National Action Committee on the Status of Women (NAC), through its Priority Campaign, For Women's Equality and Democracy: Bread and Roses, Jobs and Justice.

It is important to acknowledge the hard work of the many women who made this project possible. Many hours of unpaid and paid work have gone into the development of this valuable resource for women, our families and communities.

The Priority Campaign Committee Co-chair, Nandita Sharma, in particular must be singled out for the countless volunteer hours she gave to the project. For this we pay special tribute to her involvement. Also, members of NAC's Priority Campaign Committee, NAC Executive Committee members, women from NAC member groups, Friends of NAC, allied organizations and other individuals contributed in many ways to the voters' guide. Finally, NAC has a relatively small paid staff. They too went above the call of duty in their involvement. Laura Cabarrocas, NAC's Information Officer, tirelessly worked to input information, stay on top of the federal parties' responses and was most helpful in general trouble-shooting tasks.

NAC's Priority Campaign Committee members:
Cecile Cassista, Co-chair; Nandita Sharma, Co-chair; Joan Grant-Cummings, President; Sunera Thobani, past President; Sungee John, Laurell Ritchie, Leah Vosko, Colleen Hua, Fay Blaney, Jennifer Chew, Cenen Bagon, Bobbie Harrington, Meenu Sikand, Vuyiswa Keyi, Pam Sayne

NAC Executive Committee members:
Joan Grant-Cummings, Sunera Thobani, Cecile Cassista, Marianne Roy, Vuyiswa Keyi, Fay Blaney, Amy Go, Meenu

Sikand, Jane Robinson, Carol Ferguson, Carolann Wright, Ann Drake, Anne Kettenbcil, Bobbie Harrington, Sungee John, Kathy Mallet, Kripa Sekhar, Maureen Trotter, Florence Hackett, Melissa Munn, Sandra Head, Cenen Bagon, Nandita Sharma, Jennifer Chew, Jon Leah Hopkins

NAC staff members:
 Sandra Carnegie-Douglas, Executive Coordinator; Laura Cabarrocas, Information Officer; Tsehai Ghebremedhin, Financial Officer; Hong Hungh, Financial Data Processing Officer; Michele Havens, Data Base, Communications Systems and Membership Officer; Joanne Abbensetts, Resource Development Officer

Members of NAC, friends of NAC, allies and helpful individuals:
 Barbara Cameron, Martha Friendly, Indra Beharrysingh, Lee Lakeman, Eileen Morrow (Ontario Association of Interval and Transition Houses, OAITH), Lorraine Michael, Monica Townson, Jo-Ann Hannah, Ruth Rose, Anna Demetrakopoulos, Marie White, Sharon McIvor (Native Women's Association of Canada-NWAC), Susan Basilli, Giselle Cole, the National Anti-Poverty Organization (NAPO), GROOTS Canada, Advocacy Research Centre for Handicapped (ARCH), End Legislated Poverty (ELP), Voices for Justice in Housing, St. John's, Newfoundland, Co-operative Housing Federation of Canada, Newfoundland Amazon Network, Equality for Gays and Lesbians Everywhere (EGALE), Carissima Mathen, Maneesha Dackha, Gay Bell, Cynthia Pay, Marcia James, Kim Pate, Fiona Miller.

Preface

"Women's empowerment and their full participation on the basis of equality in all spheres of society, including participation in the decision-making process and access to power, are fundamental for the achievement of equality, development and peace."

Statement from the Beijing Platform for Action, para. 13, signed by Canada at the Fourth United Nations Conference on Women

This is the second voters' guide developed by NAC. We hope it will assist women, their families and communities in analyzing the critical issues that need to be addressed by our federal government. NAC is strongly opposed to the devolution of responsibility for social programs to the provinces. While firmly supporting the right of the people of Quebec and Aboriginal peoples to have social programs be the responsibility of governments directly controlled by them, NAC favours a strong role for the federal government in social programs for the rest of the country. The current trend towards abdicating national standards for social programs while simultaneously gutting their funding bodes ill for women. We believe that this move seriously undermines women's struggle for equality and threatens people's democratic access to decision-making in Canada.

Now more than ever, NAC speaks out firmly for the principles of social inclusion and the objective of ensuring the collective good that our national social programs, in part, embody. The existence of public social programs and services is a tribute to the past struggles of women in Canada. They represent the acknowledgement by society that the

welfare of our communities is a collective responsibility —
not one to be borne solely by individual women labouring in
isolation. Contrary to those intent on destroying the public
programs, NAC defines "welfare" positively. Among other
things, welfare means good health, social inclusion, collective accountability and general happiness.

In this voters' guide, we have highlighted important areas
of concern to women and asked for answers to questions that
hold great meaning for whether women achieve equality.
Women are currently faced with the choice of a governing
party which has racked up a lengthy list of broken promises,
federal parties spouting overt discriminatory values and social exclusion and federal parties that do not always see the
centrality and importance of the equality of women to their
party platform.

*The National Action Committee on the Status of Women's
Voters' Guide* outlines the policy positions of the five federal
political parties — the ruling Liberal Party (Liberals), the
Bloc Québécois (Bloc), the Reform Party (Reform), the New
Democratic Party (NDP) and the Progressive Conservative
Party (Tories) — on questions raised by members of NAC
through our policy committees. As the reader will see, the
responses from these federal parties is uneven, in terms of
both the questions the parties chose to respond to and the
depth of their responses. We did not generally receive responses to our questions from the Liberal Party. Therefore,
we have instead often presented the Liberal government's
record while in power, since it is their record that they are
accountable for. To supplement the parties' responses, we
also consulted the parties' latest policy documents: "Designing a Blueprint for Canadians: Guiding Principles and Policy
Priorities of the Progressive Conservative Party of Canada,"
1996 and "A Fresh Start for Canadians," by the Reform Party
of Canada, 1996. All quotes that appear in the appropriate
sections are from these official documents, unless otherwise
noted. In some instances, we draw on newspaper articles and
these are referred to following the quote. We have also
consulted media reports of statements from representatives

of different parties. Finally, in our search for answers, we have availed ourselves of the incredible depth of expertise offered by activists in the women's movement.

Issues we have highlighted include the Canada Health and Social Transfer (CHST) and NAC's call for a Canada Social Security Act; the devolution of federal responsibilities to the provinces; issues faced by Aboriginal women; immigrants, refugees and migrant workers; women with disabilities; lesbians; health and the environment; violence against women; childcare; pensions; women and work; justice policy; housing policy; post-secondary education; and women's international solidarity and foreign policy.

Many sections are introduced with a story of a woman from one of the regions of Canada and all offer an analytic summary of the issues from a feminist perspective. Each section was prepared by a woman or by women working on the corresponding policy committees of NAC. For consistency, we have tried to use the same framework throughout. We have also tried to provide an inclusive and integrated analysis of women's lives with regard to gender, racism, class, dis/ability, age and sexual orientation. We have also included a brief overview of the situation of funding for women's organizations and feminist research. We have appended the often asked for resource "Women's Guide to All Candidates' Meetings." How to get involved in NAC and be a part of the fight for women's equality and democracy is also included.

Our greatest hope is that this voters' guide will act as both a useful election tool and a call to action for holding our governments democratically accountable to women in our struggle for equality. Women demand that governments make their process transparent and that we have real public participation in decision-making!

We end with these simple but eloquent words by civil rights activist Rosa Parks: "[The time had come] when I had been pushed as far as I could stand to be pushed ... I had decided that I would have to know once and for all what rights I had as a human being ..."

Introduction

Nandita Sharma and
Joan Grant-Cummings

Since the last Canadian federal election in 1993, women have experienced serious and sustained attacks. Not only has the Liberal government of Jean Chrétien failed to make women's equality a top priority, but every social, political and economic indicator shows that there has been a growth in women's inequality — a large part of it directly as a result of the political choices this government has made. Poverty has increased for both women and their children, turning on its head the adage "women and children first."

The gap between rich and poor has grown substantially since the last federal election. Unemployment, under-employment and unregulated, unprotected jobs have all grown. The wage gap, which measures the difference in earnings between women and men, has increased for the first time in 30 years. There remains a big gap between policy and action in the area of Employment Equity and these policies are under threat of elimination or have been eliminated in many parts of the country. Likewise, pay equity gains are in peril. However, discrimination against women continues to exist in hiring, pay and promotions. Male violence against women continues unabated.

The federal government has ignored the many ways in which it could act to bring about women's equality. Instead, it has taken an active role in scapegoating specific communities (Aboriginal peoples, immigrants and refugees, people of colour, single mothers and lesbians and gays, for example) for its own disastrous record on delivering jobs and justice for women. Its employment and immigration policies appear to be based on the assumption that people deliberately choose to draw social assistance or to remain unemployed. The Liberal government has continued in the direction of the previous Tory government by shredding the Canadian social safety net and deregulating labour market protections for workers. In the process, the very mechanisms — social programs and services — that served to narrow the divide between the "haves" and the "have-nots" have come under the knife.

The Great Give-Away

The current Liberal government has blatantly abdicated its responsibility for ensuring national standards for social programs and services by slashing transfer payments to the provinces. Transfer payments are direct payments that the federal government makes to the provinces to ensure some semblance of national standards by reducing the differences between rich and poor regions. When the federal government slashes those payments, it gives the provinces a ready-made excuse to deny people their right to much-needed social programs. There has been a cut of $7 billion in federal payments for social assistance, healthcare and postsecondary education in the last two years, with more than $3.2 billion to be cut from federal cash transfers to provinces in the next two years. The results?

Medicare Threatened

Our public, universal healthcare system has been seriously undermined so that existing benefits do not cover many required services and treatments. Across the country, hospitals are being shut down. Nurses and other healthcare providers are being laid off. Women are left scrambling to find adequate homecare for disabled or sick family members and are increasingly forced into doing this care-giving work themselves. In addition, women's own health concerns continue to be ignored by governments and the medical establishment.

No Jobs

Despite the Liberal promise of "Jobs, Jobs, Jobs!" the unemployment rate has hit the double digit mark several times since 1993. This has especially hurt women in historically oppressed groups. For Aboriginal women, the official unemployment rate is 17.7 percent, although on-Reserve unemployment rates are regularly 30 percent to 80 percent for women. For women with disabilities, the unemployment rate is 19.1 percent and for women of colour it is 13.4 percent. Young women suffer from the highest unemployment rates of all, which bodes ill for our future. If we include those who have simply been discouraged from looking for work, the unemployment rate for young women is approximately 20 percent.

Yet, the number of unemployed workers who can collect unemployment insurance (UI) has dropped — from 86.8 percent in 1990 to only 51.7 percent in 1995. At the same time, the type of jobs people are able to find are lower paid, increasingly part time, unregulated and very insecure. Women have accounted for most of the increase in part-time work and most of the loss in full-time work.

What has the government's response been? Well, for a long time, the Liberals kept telling us to wait for interest rates to fall, because lower interest rates would encourage private sector employers to hire new workers. However, by the end of 1996, after 18 months of consecutive falling interest rates, the unemployment rate remained stuck at 10 percent. What we are witnessing is a "jobless recovery" as layoff notices keep being passed out despite record-high corporate profits.

Cuts = No National Standards

Despite growing unemployment and insecurity, life-sustaining and life-enhancing social security programs have been gutted, resulting in reduced payments to the poorest members of Canadian society. This has been accomplished, in part, through the elimination of the Canada Assistance Plan (CAP) and its replacement with the Canada Health and Social Transfer (CHST) in 1996. The CAP guaranteed the right to assistance that took into account a person's budgetary requirements. The CAP also made it illegal for governments to force people to work or train for welfare and gave them the right to appeal decisions.

With its decision to bring in the CHST, the Liberal government has thrown national standards out the window and stripped away the few rights to financial security that were guaranteed to people. By slashing social programs and the few economic rights we once had, the federal government has set the stage for corporate profits to take priority over the collective good. What we have left is an increasingly decentralized Canada that leaves people largely unprotected from unemployment, poverty and ill-health. As a result, many provinces are erecting or considering "residency requirements" that will deny people from outside of these provinces access to much-needed social services and programs.

Divide and Conquer: The Young and Old

One of the more insidious notions promoted by the right is intergenerational blaming. The right is encouraging young people to scapegoat seniors for their plight and encouraging seniors to be fearful of the young. Young people are told that seniors are to blame for their insecurity. There has been a recent spate of scholarly articles as well as comments from government officials that falsely suggest that older people are living in luxury from their pension payments while young people are forced to pay into a system that will not exist when they become seniors. This is nothing less than pitting one generation against another while taking the pressure off those government and corporate policies that have made both seniors and young people insecure.

Seniors have been made more insecure as public pensions come under attack. The estimated 350,000 seniors in Canada over the age of 65 with incomes between $5,000 and $15,000 who live alone and receive over 80 percent of their income from government transfers are especially vulnerable to public policy changes that affect seniors' services and benefits.

The economic status of seniors has deteriorated in the 1990s. One in five seniors continues to live in poverty. For women the figure is much worse. Women's Canada Pension Plan/Quebec Pension Plan benefits are, on average, only 58.8 percent of men's benefits, resulting in a shocking 44 percent of all senior women living in poverty. Instead of improving this situation, the Liberal government is discussing ending the universality of Old Age Security. Women stand to lose the most under the government's proposed new "Seniors Benefit," because this would eliminate women's right to independent access to pensions by tying in their entitlements to the income of their spouse.

At the same time, young people have had their futures robbed by high unemployment rates, decreasing social services, lower wages and rising university and college tuition fees. One Ontario survey found that children in Grades 5 and 6 are "worried about getting jobs when they leave school, are gloomy about a polluted world and insecure about their hopes, dreams and financial prospects"! The number of children living in poverty has increased by 46 percent since 1989. Canada now has the second highest rate of poverty among children in the Northern countries.

Rising tuition fees have been an additional blow to the young. Tuition fees for universities have shot up 75 percent since 1982 while federal funding for postsecondary education has been reduced by 26 percent. This has meant that the financial debt carried by students in Canada has grown dramatically. As a result, student numbers dropped in 1995 — the first time enrollment has declined since 1978.

Crisis of Poverty

As a result of fewer jobs, lower earnings and falling social assistance and UI payments, there is a crisis of poverty in this country. This is especially true for people within historically discriminated-against groups, such as Aboriginal women, women of colour and women with disabilities.

According to Statistics Canada, at the end of 1996, a total of 5.2 million — or one in six — people in Canada lived in poverty. This represents an increase of 264,000 people from 1994! Four of ten children — or 1.5 million children — live below the poverty line. This figure represents a 45 percent increase since 1989 when the House of Commons vowed to eliminate the poverty of children by the year 2000. If all these children live in poverty, we can be sure their mothers are living in poverty too. High rates of unemployment, low wages and cuts to social assistance leave these families without any options. Most telling about the status of women in Canada is the statistic that almost 61 percent of all families living in poverty are households headed by single mothers.

Again, boding ill for our future, almost two-thirds of young adults under 25 years are now poor. While we hear much from both the provinces and the federal government about the need to end child poverty, the most they are prepared to do about it is to merge the money now being spent by two levels of government on a variety of programs into one "new" program created "within existing fiscal frameworks" to be jointly managed. And this, they say, is "doing something" about child poverty.

Scapegoating and Poor-Bashing Tactics

To make matters worse, the federal government and other political parties are at the forefront of scapegoating campaigns directed at blaming single mothers, the poor, the unemployed, immigrants, refugees and young people. Aboriginal peoples, people of colour, people with disabilities, lesbians and seniors have also been cast as villains supposedly responsible for the collective economic and social insecurity that many people in Canada face.

For instance, we are told that the reason so many people rely upon social assistance is not the failure of society to acknowledge the social contributions of women's unpaid work or the failure of the government to provide a national childcare program but because welfare is "addictive" and leads to "dependency." This is an incredibly convenient excuse for governments intent on remaining unaccountable for the social and economic policies they have brought in. When the rich get tax breaks and deductions, we don't hear the same complaints about the wealthy being "dependent" on tax payers!

The scapegoating of Aboriginal people, immigrants, the poor, the unemployed, and the young has let governments (and the corporations backing them) off the hook. Instead, the public's understandable anger at increasing levels of unemployment and poverty has been misdirected at those who are already the poorest and most vulnerable in Canada. This strategy, jointly conceived by the government and Big Business, is turning our society into a more mean-spirited one and preventing us from progressing in our fight for equality.

Is There No Alternative?

Contributing to the crisis is the fact that we have been told by our government and by the increasingly concentrated corporate-owned media that this is the reality that women must accept. Often heard through the corridors of power — whether in the House of Commons or in corporate boardrooms — is the refrain, "There is no alternative." Ever since coming to power, the Liberal government has joined in this destructive and decidedly undemocratic chorus.

As a result, much of the destruction wreaked on women's lives has been done in the name of deficit reduction. Prime Minister Chrétien keeps saying that his job is to get the nation's books in order. He is one of those telling us that "there is no alternative" to gutting social programs and services or laying off tens of thousands of public sector workers.

However, Doug Peters, who was appointed by Chrétien to study the deficit, estimates that less than 10 percent of the deficit results from social spending while 50 percent results from revenue shortfalls and 40 percent from high interest rates. In fact, in 1993, 93,000 profit-making corporations paid no taxes at all!

Nobel Prize–winning economist William Vickrey states quite simply that "the insane pursuit of the holy grail of a balanced budget in the end is going to drive the economy into depression." (See *Toronto Star*, October 27, 1996, "Two cities, two manners of indifference to the public.") Finally, even the government's own Finance Committee has said that the government should shift its focus from deficit cutting to doing something concrete to end poverty. Yet, the Liberal government continues to place "balancing the books" before all else.

Federal cutbacks in social spending have dramatically reduced the state's role in redistributing income from the wealthy to the less well-off. Indeed, one of the victories of the right is that they have convinced some people that only social assistance or UI payments constitute "welfare" in Canada. What they would like us to believe is that corporate tax deferrals, business "entertainment" deductions and tax loopholes are not a form of welfare to those who are well-off.

In fact, the majority of government spending (including the foregoing of federal revenues through tax breaks) is spent on those who are not poor and most often very wealthy. Corporate tax rates in Canada are the lowest rate of corporate contributions to public revenue in all G-7 countries and corporate taxes in Canada are already among the lowest in the countries of the North. There have been $40 billion in deferred corporate taxes since 1993. Banks and trust and insurance companies alone enjoyed $5 billion of untaxed profits since 1994 — despite record breaking billion dollar profits.

What is most telling is the change in the share of federal revenue coming from either individual or corporate taxes. In 1984, less than 50 percent of federal revenue came from individuals while about 15 percent came from corporations. In 1994, the share of federal revenue coming from individuals jumped by almost 10 percent, to almost 60 percent while the share of corporate contributions decreased to less than

10 percent! Increasing personal taxes (through changes in the income tax laws or through regressive taxes like the hated GST) have led to the scapegoating of welfare recipients by those who resent paying more and getting less. Attention has successfully been diverted away from the wealthy who benefit from federal revenues.

Perhaps no other group in society exemplifies this inequity better than the big banks. In 1996, the Big Six banks alone raked in a profit of over $6 billion dollars — up 22 percent from their whopping profits of 1995.

Zeroing in on slashing social programs and the public sector while ignoring the billions lost to the federal government through tax breaks or deferrals to the rich and corporate elite is clearly a serious mistake — if getting rid of the deficit and debt is really the main priority.

Cheap Labour and Big Private Profits

Because focusing on spending cuts instead of ways to increase much needed revenues as a strategy to reduce the deficit is so ill-advised, we suspect that another motive is at play. NAC believes that a number of related strategies are at work, all aimed at increasing the profits and power of corporations through the employment of a cheap labour strategy that ultimately undermines democracy and destroys the women's movement equality agenda.

The deregulation of the labour market and union-busting activities coupled with high unemployment rates and shrinking social programs or services have left people more vulnerable to the demands of employers — whether for longer work hours, less pay, fewer or no benefits — and to sexual and racist harassment. The increased transfer of federal responsibilities for social programs to provinces and territories and the abdication of the duty to maintain national standards have exacerbated this growing trend of increasing the powers of employers. Employers benefit when different regions of the country or different social groups can be pitted against one another to create the cheapest labour force possible.

These changes have also threatened democracy. The growing distance between what the elites want and what the rest of us want is one clear indicator. The elites' priorities are to gut social programs and eliminate national standards, deregulate labour markets and weaken the collective bargaining rights of unions.

What People in Canada Want

There is no evidence to support the notion that people in Canada wish to entrust social services to market forces. On the contrary, polls conducted in 1996 and 1997 show that the top priorities for people in Canada are jobs and the protection of public and universal healthcare and other social programs. A recent 1996 poll showed that the majority of people in Canada "acknowledge the crucial role of the federal government in constructing our national identity," which for most people is "rooted in the activities of the federal government."

The Liberal government is not doing what people in Canada want — creating jobs and protecting national social programs. The majority in Canada has not been silent. It has been abandoned by those elected to represent our interests.

To compound the problem, private, back room deals between the federal and provincial governments have led to a situation where people have been further removed from democratically controlling our political leaders. The 1996 Premiers' Forum is a good example. The federal government used this forum to negotiate with the provinces on such important matters as the end of national standards on various social programs, child poverty and services to Aboriginal peoples without any public input! Yet, it is clear that the most popularly supported social programs, like old-age pensions and unemployment insurance, have been those with federal standards and national eligibility criteria. Cutting social program funding and simultaneously downloading power to the provinces is one sure way of killing the effectiveness of social programs and destroying the public's support.

Jobs and Justice

More and more, governments are being run like corporations. Our parliamentary democracy has increasingly assimilated the values of the private sector. Indeed, instead of democracy we have a type of corporate rule where the Prime Minister acts as if he is the Chief Executive Office (CEO) rather than the elected political leader of the people. This "government as a business" approach defines people as "customers" instead of citizens. Balancing books and focusing on ensuring the "bottom line" have been made more important than ensuring our human rights and providing both the material and the social conditions with which we can live our lives as women with dignity.

To obscure the diminishment of democracy in our lives, the right have advanced the notion that governments *per se* and not bad government policies are the problem. This has led to a climate in which people are encouraged to fight against each other and to mistrust elected representatives instead of those who undermine the quality of life in Canada. Who hasn't heard the right-wing refrain that eliminating "big government" or "politicians" will solve all our problems?

We must carefully examine the rhetoric of "downsizing government" and reducing taxes. It is only through having elected officials that we can hold our governments accountable. It is only through the federal government's spending powers that we have had national standards for social programs in the first place.

What we need to do is challenge our elected officials and make them accountable to society as a whole and not only to the corporate elites. We must resist succumbing to the right-wing notion that private markets can solve all problems. We must resist and act against any movement that takes power out of the hands of people and their elected officials.

Recently, much of this attack against democracy has been done in the guise of cutting taxes. Cutting taxes without addressing the problem that corporations do not pay their fair share of taxes will only deepen the growing disparities in income. After the tax cuts, governments will have another excuse for not providing public services.

NAC is strongly opposed to the devolution or downloading of responsibility for social programs to the provinces. While firmly supporting the right of the people of Quebec and Aboriginal peoples to make social programs the responsibility of the governments directly controlled by them, NAC favours a strong role for the federal government in social programs for the rest of the country. What we need is a *strong* federal government — not a weakened one — to maintain the standards and protective measures that people affirm over and over are essential values within our society. We need to struggle for a society where people, through the use of their democratically elected governments, act to improve their lives and ensure equality. This is what we want for ourselves and our communities and this is what we want for our sisters throughout the world.

A recent poll showed that women more than men are concerned with the gutting of the social safety net and the destruction of Medicare and social assistance. The gender gap between policies women support and ones men support has remained strong and constant. This is because women are usually the ones who pick up the pieces of destroyed public services in order to meet the needs of their families and communities.

When governments attack the very institutions, programs and services that women in Canada continually call for, we cannot fail to identify this as a dismissal of our demands and an attack against our equality rights. Since the last federal election, the federal government has failed to hear our concerns about equality. We have been sidelined and far removed from the decisions and decision-making processes that have major effects on our lives.

Women's Equality and Democracy

The stakes are clearly too high for any one of us to be a spectator to governance. Governing is not a spectator sport. It is government policies and practices that shape whether we live

in poverty or have jobs with a future. It is government policies and practices that shape whether we will have access to
safe, affordable, public childcare and whether our human
rights will be protected and guaranteed.

It is our democratic right to hold our government accountable, to challenge our elected officials and to push them to
act in a way that respects women's equality and democracy.
The federal government acts on our behalf. We must not
forget that we put them there and that we can toss them out
— through voting.

Voting is a right that we still have and we must use it well.
We cannot buy into the defeatist notion that "there is no alternative." There are choices to be made. It serves the agendas of
the corporate elite to foster apathy among members of the
public, a sense of powerlessness, a feeling of being over-
whelmed, "turned off" and unhappy with the system.

We need to recognize that a society that no longer has
faith in its democratic processes will be more easily subjected to being led down a path that is fundamentally in
opposition to a women's equality agenda. Opting out is dangerous. Now, more than ever, a call to action to create and
sustain social equality is essential and this call must be
answered by all of us.

Inspired by the Quebec Women's March for Bread and
Roses, NAC and the Canadian Labour Congress (CLC) answered this call in 1996 when we organized the largest
grassroots mobilization of women in Canadian history — the
Women's March Against Poverty: For Bread and Roses,
Jobs and Justice. We went into over 100 communities from
coast to coast to coast. Over 100,000 women participated in
March events and thousands more made their voices heard
in other ways. Fifteen demands designed to help eliminate
women's poverty were put to the Prime Minister. The March
culminated in a rally on Parliament Hill in Ottawa attended
by about 50,000 people. This massive mobilization was not
the only objective of the March, however.

Women are increasingly recognizing the need to develop
a long-term plan for how we will increase our meaningful

participation (as opposed to a token one) in the electoral process. It was acknowledged that the implementation of a Woman's Equality Agenda for Social Justice must be integral to our strategy, our political choices and our actions. We have within the women's equality movement the potential to develop an economic, social and political model based upon equality and democracy.

1

A Canada Social
Security Act

Nandita Sharma

---

*While we were on the Women's March Against Poverty, a
worker at a battered women's shelter told us of a woman
who had fled Saskatchewan. This woman was trying to escape an abusive husband. She went to British Columbia
thinking that her husband would have difficulty finding her
there and approached the Ministry of Social Services for
financial assistance. She wanted to recover from the trauma
of abuse, find accommodation, and a job and live her life
without male violence. But, because she had not lived in BC
for three months, she was not considered a resident of the
province and was refused assistance by the provincial government. She was left with nothing to eat. She had nowhere
to live. She had no one to turn to. And so she returned to
Saskatchewan ... She represents too many women.*

NAC and the Canadian Labour Congress
Demand

We demand a Canada Social Security Act! We call on the
government to bring in a Canada Social Security Act to
restore the four fundamental national standards for social
assistance and to add a fifth standard prohibiting discrimination in the design and delivery of programs and services.

Replacement of the Canada Assistance Plan with the Canada Health and Social Transfer

On April 1, 1996, the federal government replaced the Canada Assistance Plan (CAP) with the Canada Health and Social Transfer (CHST). The CHST redefines the roles of all levels of government in Canada in the funding and delivery of social programs. While firmly supporting the right of the people of Quebec and Aboriginal peoples to have their governments directly control their social programs, NAC favours a strong role for the federal government in social programs for the rest of the country.

The CHST represents the biggest change to social policy in decades. It has wiped out the minimum rights that people in Canada had to social assistance. With the replacement of CAP with the CHST, we have lost

1. the right to social assistance based solely on need,

2. the right to not be forced to participate in work-for-welfare or train-for-welfare programs,

3. the right to an adequate level of income (this level would take into account such basic needs as clothing, food, housing, fuel, utilities, household supplies, childcare, personal needs and support services),

4. the right to appeal decisions made about a person's social assistance entitlement.

The only right we formally have left is the right to collect social assistance in any province no matter how long we have lived there. Yet, even this right was ignored by the British Columbia government until March 1997. The residency restriction was finally removed after the government responded to a BC Supreme Court decision that ruled it as illegal.

The CHST gets rid of national standards for social assistance, health care and postsecondary education. It represents a major leap backwards for women in Canada.

With the CHST, the Liberals have already cut federal transfers — the money the federal government gives the provinces — for social programs by over $7 billion. By the year 2000, the Liberals will have cut $11.1 billion, giving the provinces a made-in-Ottawa excuse for attacking the poor. Already many of the provinces have put measures into place that are devastating to those relying on social assistance.

Workfare in Canada

An example of the havoc being caused in people's lives is the establishment of "work-for-welfare" or "train-for-welfare" programs. These workfare programs could not have been imposed under the Canada Assistance Plan. CAP guaranteed the right to social assistance without the recipient having to work or train for benefits.

Many municipalities in Ontario have mandatory workfare programs and other provinces have variations such as the Youth Works and Welfare to Work programs in BC, the Alberta Community Economic Development (ACED) program in Alberta, the New Brunswick Works program in New Brunswick and the so-called "top-up" program for social assistance recipients in Quebec that recruits workers for businesses that have registered with the provincial government. Women in all of these provinces have borne the brunt of these programs.

Many people think workfare is a good idea. ("After all, I have to work for my living, why shouldn't they?") In fact, there are many problems with work-for-welfare and train-for-welfare programs.

One concern is that governments and corporations have laid off union workers and replaced them with social assistance recipients coerced into taking these jobs. So, relatively decent jobs are being lost and wages and working conditions are being driven downwards. These "workfare" programs are clearly part of the government's low-wage strategy to convert our workforce into a more "flexible," "competitive" and, ultimately, cheaper one that is forced to compete internationally with people in poorer countries who historically have been made to accept the lowest of wages. Clearly, this is a race to the bottom. The only winners are those who own the businesses relying on cheap labour.

Employers rarely hire workers at the end of the workfare programs, so that the programs operate as a subsidy to business, paid for by the tax payer, with no requirement to actually provide stable employment at decent wages for people.

These programs are punitive. They punish welfare recipients for not having a job. But recipients *do* want to work and receive training. The reality is that jobs that pay a living wage are scarce. Unemployment is over 10 percent nationally and is much higher in many regions. Most newly created jobs are low paying and part time and without benefits or security. Childcare spaces are scarce and often unaffordable. Few people, especially women supporting children, can survive on these jobs.

In order to provide meaningful training for careers that pay a living wage (rather than job search skills taught in the current training programs), the cost to the government would be significant. Instead of making this investment, the federal government is cutting funding to postsecondary education. Funding for postsecondary education, decent minimum wage laws to provide a real alternative to welfare and redistribution of work time, not "workfare," are the keys to getting people out of poverty.

The Poor Are under Attack

The CHST is based on a Charity Model instead of a Rights Model of social assistance. The CHST promotes the idea that only some people who are poor are "deserving" of our assistance. This translates into the dangerous belief that some people deserve to be poor and that poverty, instead of being a social problem, is a problem resting with the individual. These attitudes make it easier to scapegoat and target the poor for attacks. Both historically and in the present, women have been thought of as undeserving more often than men. Women who are single mothers, Aboriginal women, women of colour and women with disabilities have been particularly targetted.

The following is a brief review of the situation of people who require social assistance in the ten provinces. The statistics/information in this section have been provided, in part, by the National Anti-Poverty Organization (NAPO).

British Columbia

- Social assistance benefits cut by 8 percent for people and families classified "employable."

- Single parents considered employable when the youngest child reaches 7 (previously 12).

- Three-month-residency requirement cuts (eliminated only in March 1997).

- Youth Works Program mandatory for employable youth ages 19 to 24 to be eligible for benefits.

- Welfare to Work program imposed for employable adults 25 and older.

- Closure of 14 welfare offices across BC has eliminated both services and jobs.

Alberta

- Basic social assistance rates cut by 13 percent for single employable people and families.

- Drug coverage limited to life-sustaining generic drugs only.

- ACED program stipulates that those who don't participate can be cut off benefits.

Saskatchewan

- Social assistance rates unchanged since the 1980s.

- Social assistance recipients are required to apply for Canada Pension Plan (CPP) early retirement (reduced) benefits at age 60 (previously 65).

- "New Careers" is a 20-week subsidized employment program.

Manitoba

- Social assistance rates cut by 10 percent for employable singles and couples without children.

- Reductions of 2 percent made to overall budget for single-parent families.

- Parents considered employable when youngest child reaches 6.

- As of September 16, 1996, Bill C-36 was tabled before the legislature. If passed, it would remove the previous clause that ensured that there was a legal obligation to provide social assistance benefits where a person would otherwise lack basic necessities.

- Bill C-36 would also force social assistance recipients to develop a "case plan" for participation in an employment or training program; benefits can be cut if the plan is not followed.

Ontario

- $8 billion cut in social program spending.

- Social assistance rates cut by 21.6 percent for everyone but people with disabilities and seniors.

- The term disability has been re-defined to exclude many previously covered, resulting in many people with disabilities having to live with fewer resources.

- Funding to community-based agencies cut.

- New $2 fee charged for prescriptions.

- More supervision of the poor. There has been a major re-definition of the term "common-law spouse" so that two people of the opposite sex living together are defined as common-law from the moment they move in together. Those deemed to be "common-law" are now unable to collect welfare as a single person or parent. Home visits by social workers are now a condition of eligibility.

- More stringent conditions for welfare eligibility applied to youth aged 16 to 17.

- An "employable" person who is forced to quit a job must wait three months before applying for welfare.

- Postsecondary students are unable to collect welfare except in "special" circumstances.

- Mandatory workfare (Ontario Works) requirements are in place in many municipalities.

Quebec

- Monthly rate paid to those "available but not participating" in an employment program reduced by $50.

- Monthly rate paid to those participating in an employment program reduced by $30.

- Social assistance benefit rates change depending on whether people are classified as "non-available," "participating" or "non-participating" in designated employability development programs; monthly penalties range between $150 and $300.

- Social assistance recipients must pay 25 percent of their prescriptions to a maximum of $200/year.

New Brunswick

- Welfare rates are the lowest in Canada (maximum single employable rate is $260/month; single-parent rate is $880 to $929/month depending on child's age).

- Attendance in school or training programs for youth aged 16 to 21 is mandatory.

- "Social assessment" for youth aged 16 to 18 before receipt of social assistance is mandatory.

- Ability to share residence is severely curtailed. Only one person classified as a *single* "employable" in a household is eligible to receive social assistance.

- Claimants are required to apply for early CPP benefits at ages 60 to 64.

- Social assistance recipients are "highly encouraged" to take placements in New Brunswick Works or Job Corps, the province's employment programs.

Nova Scotia

- Shelter rates for single employable recipients cut by 36 percent (from $350 to $225/month).

- Single parents must pay $3 per prescription to qualify for assistance; the maximum paid by social assistance capped at $150 annually.

Prince Edward Island

- Shelter rates in urban areas reduced by 36.5 percent (from $480 to $305/month).

- Shelter rates in rural areas reduced by 36.6 percent (from $410 to $260/month).

- GST tax credit no longer exempt in calculation of benefits.

Newfoundland

- Home support care reduced by 10 percent, with certain exceptions.

- $3 pharmacy dispensing fee imposed per prescription.

- "Top up" of $61 eliminated in certain circumstances (for example, payment of utility expenses).

- User fees for school buses imposed.

- Health cuts imposed, including limited dental payments, reduced number of drugs or medical supplies and decreased transportation assistance for medical appointments and treatments.

- Income tax rebate clawback for all recipients imposed.

Information on the Yukon and the Northwest Territories is not available.

The Need for a Canada Social Security Act

NAC's position is that Canada needs a Canada Social Security Act to replace the CHST.

Not only are women most negatively affected by the CHST, but we are most in danger of living in poverty as a result of it. The CHST represents an attack upon our equality rights. For women, cuts in social services mean an increase in poverty. It represents a threat to our ability to leave situations where we experience male violence. It means an increase in our unpaid domestic work. It means a loss of better paid jobs within the public sector.

The "feminization of poverty'" is increasing as a result of government public program policies, trade policies and the deregulation of the labour market. Statistics do not convey the daily realities of the women they represent. Yet, the statistics do give us some indication of the scope and seriousness of the issue of poverty facing women in Canada.

Women currently experience the highest rates of poverty in Canada. The percentage of women living in poverty is consistently higher than that of men. Women make up the majority of minimum wage earners who rely on social assistance at some time during the year. Women are more often found in temporary, contract employment positions than are men. The number of jobs in the so-called "precarious sector" (that is, homework) is rapidly increasing. The majority of workers in this sector are women.

The CHST strips people living in poverty of their rights of citizenship and creates a group of people in Canada left without hope and means to escape a life of poverty. We are already witnessing a loss in the status of women as a result of the change from CAP to CHST.

With the CHST has come a change in attitude. Sole-support mothers who require social assistance are subjected to vicious attacks on their right to raise their children on their own. Women with disabilities are portrayed as "burdens" upon society. Aboriginal women are described as "dependent" on "tax payers." Immigrant women and women of colour are scapegoated for declining living standards. Older women are being defined as a drain on future generations and lesbians as a threat to "family values."

These changes are not happening on their own. Occurring at the same time is the erosion of healthy community values — the provision of universal, public services. The right wing

want us to hear the term "welfare" as derogatory and insult-
ing. It has become associated with dependency and social
irresponsibility.

But women define "welfare" positively. For us it means
equality, good health, general happiness and well-being.
Women have always had to struggle to get all of society
involved in caring for each other. Women have said that it
is not socially responsible to deny healthcare or education to
people. It is not socially responsible to deny admittance to
immigrants to Canada because they don't have enough in
their bank accounts. Women have been fighting for the rights
of all people, including children, to social rights — not
handouts!

NAC shares the vision of a Canada Social Security Act
where the four national standards for social assistance eliminated by the CHST are restored. To these NAC adds another
standard: no discrimination in the design and delivery of
programs and services.

The Canada Social Security Act would ensure that the
provinces respect the following five basic social rights:

1. The right of any person in need in Canada to an adequate level of income. This amount would take into account
such basic needs as clothing, food, housing, fuel, utilities,
household supplies, childcare, personal needs and support
services.

2. The right to social assistance based solely on need.
People should not be forced to participate in community
work, work-for-welfare or train-for-welfare programs.

3. The right to appeal administrative decisions related to
a person's social assistance entitlement.

4. The right to assistance no matter how long a person has
lived in a province.

5. The right to assistance without discrimination in the
design or delivery of programs and services. Discrimination
based on sex, race, national or ethnic background, sexual
orientation, religion, age or mental or physical disability
should be illegal.

The Act must require the federal government to enforce these standards. This should be done through stable, significant cash transfers to the provinces. The formula used for these transfers must be responsive to changes in demand for benefits. These changes in demand may be the result of increases in population and/or economic conditions. At the same time, NAC supports the right of the people of Quebec and of Aboriginal peoples to control their own social programs. An opting-out clause may be needed to meet their concerns while insuring compliability for the rest of the country.

Question:

Where do the political parties stand on the Canada Social Security Act?

Liberal Party (Liberals)
The Liberals' record shows they do not support our version of a Canada Social Security Act.

- Since 1993, the Liberals have scrapped four of the five rights ensured by the Canada Assistance Plan and replaced CAP with CHST;

- The Liberals have also cut transfer payments to the provinces for social assistance, health and postsecondary education by $7 billion in the last two years. By the year 2000, the Liberals will have slashed $11.1 billion from federal transfers for social programs. These actions have given the provinces a ready-made excuse to deny people social assistance;

- At the Fall 1996 Liberal Party Convention a resolution was passed supporting a different version of a Canada Social Security Act. The original proposal called for the federal government to guarantee national standards for the whole social safety net, including Medicare. The version accepted by the

Liberal Party only agreed to the guarantee of standards negotiated between the provinces and the federal government.

Bloc Québécois (Bloc)
The Bloc support the five fundamental social rights of the Canada Social Security Act and its creation for "the rest of Canada," excluding Quebec (where the Quebec government would have exclusive jurisdiction over social programs).

Reform Party (Reform)
The Reform Party does not support a Canada Social Security Act.

A Reform government would abdicate all federal responsibility for ensuring national standards for social assistance by "restoring welfare to provincial and local governments."

Reform would cut all the $3.5 billion in transfers to the provinces for welfare programs such as Meals on Wheels, homemaker services for seniors, attendant services for people with disabilities, childcare, protection for abused children, battered women's shelters, and provision of wheelchairs.

In fact, Reform would cut $15 billion a year from federal funding and reduce taxes ensuring that there are no national programs or standards.

Reform would also cut equalization payments to the poorer provinces by $3 billion a year. This would mean that people in these provinces would face cuts in social services and healthcare.

New Democratic Party (NDP)
The NDP support the concept of a Canada Social Security Act.

The NDP are on record as opposing the massive cuts made to federal transfers to social programs. The NDP believe that "all Canadians" are entitled

to a minimal standard of income protection in spite
of inequalities in the fiscal capacity of their province of residence.

Progressive Conservative Party (Tories)
The Tories do not support the creation of a Canada
Social Security Act.

They state that "national standards for social programs should no longer be dictated by the federal
government." They continue by saying that they
will "streamline" and "consolidate" all income support programs in Canada that would not be based
on universal principles but be needs-tested.

Also, the Tories are promising to cut corporate
and personal taxes by 10 to 20 percent, thereby
making it more difficult to ever create adequate social programs with national standards enforced by
the federal government's spending powers.

2

Devolution of Federal Responsibilities to the Provinces

Barbara Cameron

NAC is strongly opposed to devolving or downloading responsibility for social programs to the provinces. While firmly supporting the right of the people of Quebec and Aboriginal peoples to have their governments directly control their social programs, NAC favours a strong role for the federal government in social programs for the rest of the country.

The Downloading of Federal Powers

Many Canadians are unaware of the extent to which the Liberal government has given powers to the provinces. Indeed, the Liberals have continued the policies of the Mulroney Conservatives and in many respects have gone much further than them in reducing the federal role.

This devolution has taken place through four methods. First, the Liberals have dramatically decreased federal transfers to the provinces and territories to fund social programs. By the time the Liberals face the Canadian electorate in 1997/98, they will have slashed their funding of provincial social programs by about $7 billion since coming into office.

This is a decline of 33.5 percent. By the year 2000, the Liberals will have cut $11.1 billion from federal transfers to the provinces for social programs! Liberal candidates are likely to deny this, claiming that they have "only" cut 14.6 percent. But the basis for this claim is an accounting trick used by finance ministers, both Liberal and Conservative, to disguise the ongoing abdication of federal leadership in social programs.[1]

No Cash, No Clout

Although the Liberals often discuss "tax points" in connection with spending on social programs, cash is the only important part. As the Liberal Chair of the federal Finance Committee Jim Petersen admitted, "No cash, no clout." It is the cash that allowed the federal government to enforce the standards in the Canada Health Act when provinces were permitting doctors to extra-bill. Unless it maintains cash transfer, the federal government cannot ensure respect for Canadian standards for social programs.

The government's way of reporting federal spending on social programs amounts to nothing less than a conspiracy against the Canadian people. This reporting has allowed the Liberal government, like the Conservative government before it, to follow a strategy of "decentralization by deceit." The government has managed this sleight of hand by introducing massive cuts to the federal cash transfer, while using the predictable increases in the value of the tax points to disguise the extent of the reduction.

Under the Conservatives, the federal cash contribution to provincial social programs was slated to erode year after year until 2009, when no province would receive any federal cash for social programs. This would have left the federal government with absolutely no ability to enforce Canadian social standards.

During his 1994 and 1995 budgets, Finance Minister Paul Martin continued on exactly the same path. It was only as a result of the vigorous opposition of NAC and other organizations which support social programs, that the 1996 federal budget included a commitment that the federal cash component would not fall below $11 billion at any point before the year 2002/03. This figure still represents a decline of 41.5 percent in the federal cash transfer to the provinces for social programs since the first budget of this Liberal government!

The provincial governments have made it clear that $11 billion is not enough to justify the federal government setting Canadian standards for social programs. This is the reason provincial premiers have set in motion a process to substitute themselves for the Parliament of Canada as the institution that establishes "national" standards.

NAC has criticized the federal government for what amounts to cooking the financial books. Along with many other social policy groups and experts, we have demanded that the federal government claim only the cash it is currently giving the provinces for social programs. We are further demanding that the Liberals restore the cash transfer to the amount it was when they came into office — $18.8 billion. Finally, we are demanding that the federal government establish a formula that will ensure that the cash portion increases annually in a manner that will secure the federal role in social programs and guarantee the federal government's capacity to enforce Canadian standards for social programs.

An End to National Standards

The second way the Liberals have given away power to the provinces is through eliminating national standards for social assistance. The Canada Health and Social Transfer (CHST), which was announced in the February 1995 budget and which came into effect April 1, 1996, eliminated protections that people living in poverty had under the Canada Assistance Plan. In NAC's view, this effectively stripped poor people in Canada of social rights. By leaving in place only one standard — no residence requirements — the Liberals have built in a penalty for any province that wants to maintain adequate programs and have ensured a race to the bottom as provinces compete to lower supports to poor people (see "A Canada Social Security Act" in this guide).

The third and fourth ways the Liberals have given powers to the provinces involve introducing legislation directly borrowed from the defeated Meech Lake and Charlottetown Accords.

In its 1996 Speech from the Throne, the Liberal government voluntarily agreed not to introduce new cost-shared programs unless it had the support of seven provinces with 50 percent of the population. Since Quebec is opposed on principle to federal social programs, this formula effectively gives a veto to the Ontario government — currently headed by the Tories' Mike Harris — over federal spending on new social programs. Had this provision been in place in the sixties, there would never have been a Medicare program in Canada. It makes a national childcare act a virtual impossibility.

Finally, the federal government has withdrawn from certain areas and declared that the provinces have exclusive responsibility. These responsibilities include training, a field in which the federal government has always played a more important role than the provinces. This policy is particularly damaging to women and to disadvantaged minorities because the federal government has provided the leadership in recognizing equity principles in training.

During the Referendum on a proposed Charlottetown Accord, NAC expressed the strong opposition of the women's movement to the limitation of the federal spending power and to the federal withdrawal from social programs, such as training in the rest of Canada, while emphasizing the legitimacy of the people in Quebec to control social programs.

Question:

Where do the parties stand on ensuring a strong role for themselves and the federal government in guaranteeing national standards for social programs?

Liberal Party (Liberals)

The Liberals' record shows they do not favour a strong role for the federal government in guaranteeing national standards for social programs. Already having cut over $7 billion from federal transfers to the provinces for social programs, if re-elected they will cut a further $4 billion by the year 2000. The Liberals are abdicating their federal responsibilities by devolving power to the provinces and, therefore, eliminating national standards on social programs and services. The CHST, the erosion of national standards for immigrant/refugee settlement services and the handing over of job-training programs to the provinces are only a few examples.

Bloc Québécois (Bloc)

The Bloc consider social programs to be an exclusive provincial responsibility.

The Bloc have not supported a strong role for the federal government in guaranteeing national standards for social programs in the rest of Canada.

Reform Party (Reform)

Reform would substantially weaken the role of the federal government.

Reform favour devolution. A Reform government would decentralize federal government powers "to give all provinces the freedom and resources to develop as ... [they] choose."

Reform state that a vision of Canada based upon national programs and national standards "delivers friction, disunity, non-accountability, duplication and waste." They add that this vision "trivializes our sense of ourselves by implying that only through government programs, government spending, and government propaganda can this country be held together."

Reform would "make government smaller" by reducing the "size and tax requirements of the federal government," by cutting $15 billion a year "program by program, position by position" and by transferring "major responsibilities back to individuals, families, and communities."

Reform would also substantially reduce federal government revenues through their promise of tax cuts, making it that much more difficult to ensure social programs and services (most tax cuts would come from reducing taxes on the rich and on business owners: capital gains taxes cut in half, 5 percent surtax on high income earners eliminated, employers' Unemployment Insurance (UI) premiums cut by 28 percent and the income tax system "flattened"). In reality, if you include the promised tax cuts, Reform would actually have to cut $25 billion from the federal budget.

Reform would eliminate regional development agencies, the office of official languages, all Secretaries of State and the Canadian Radio Television and Telecommunications Commission (CRTC), and significantly reduce Canadian Heritage, Indian Affairs and Northern Development, the Canadian International Development Agency (CIDA) and the Transport department.

In addition, Reform would merge, refocus or reduce spending on Parliament and in the following departments and agencies: Finance; Foreign Affairs and International Trade; Industry; Justice and Solicitor General; National Defence; National Revenue; Public Works; Treasury Board; Privy Council Office; Citizenship and Immigration (with responsibility for immigration moved to Foreign Affairs and the Department of Justice); Human Resource Department; Agriculture; Natural Resources; and Fisheries and Oceans (the Coast Guard would be transferred to Defence).

New Democratic Party (NDP)

The NDP are in favour of a strong role for the federal government.

They believe that only at the federal level can the universality of social programs be protected.

Progressive Conservative Party (Tories)

The Tories would substantially weaken the role of the federal government. They favour devolution.

They state that "national standards for social programs should no longer be dictated by the federal government." They believe that "basic standards" should be up for negotiation between the provinces and the territories and the federal government.

The Tories would eliminate universal benefits by basing income support on "need" and linking the receipt of benefits to work, education and skills training (that is, work-for-welfare or train-for-welfare). They state that "the size of our national debt combined with the future costs of pension, health care and other programs raises serious questions about whether all these commitments can be sustained."

The Tories are calling for spending cuts, supposedly to eliminate the federal deficit. But, at the same time, they are calling for a tax cut of 10 to 20 percent, thereby ensuring that social programs would face further severe cuts and that the federal government would lose the clout it has to enforce national standards — cash! A 10 percent cut in taxes would mean $6 billion less in revenues.

In the provision of social programs and services, the Tories would emphasize "the objectives of self-reliance and self-sufficiency." They believe that "responsibility for the well-being of citizens rests first and foremost with the individual and family."

Ultimately, the Tories believe that the federal government's activities and costs should be limited by what they believe is its "appropriate role" of

"foster[ing] an environment whereby the private
sector ... [is] encouraged to invest ..."

"Forestry, mines, recreation, housing, municipal
affairs and training," the Tories state, "must be de-
volved to the provinces ...."

Endnotes

1. The way this trick works is that the federal budget counts the
value of taxes that the federal government has not collected since
1977 and that the provinces collect and spend instead as federal
spending on social programs. This is hard to believe, but true.

To understand this, think of personal income tax revenue as a
big pie, some of which is collected by the federal government and
some by the provincial governments. In 1977, the federal government decreased its portion of the pie and allowed the provinces to
increase their portion. The result was an increase in the tax revenue
controlled by the provinces with no increase in the total taxes paid
by voters. The portion of the pie transferred to the provinces is
called "tax points." The total number of tax points transferred has
not changed since 1977, but their value (the amount of tax dollars
they bring in) has. This is because the total pie — the total revenue
from personal income taxes — rises as personal incomes increase.

When federal governments talk about their spending on social
programs delivered by the provinces, they talk about two things:
the cash out of this year's budget *and* the current value of the tax
points they transferred in 1977. The cash is the only real part. The
tax points represent money that the federal government would have
had if it had not transferred tax points to the provinces in 1977! It
is in fact provincial tax revenue and virtually every politician and
government policy-maker in Canada connected to social policy
knows this.

3

Aboriginal Women

Fay Blaney

NAC was told of a young Métis woman who had been desperately looking for work in the city of Winnipeg. She had moved from a small community in northern Alberta to escape a violent relationship. She had no family in Winnipeg. The woman decided to upgrade her education. After a few months of attending an adult education program, she dropped out due to the racism she experienced. Her welfare worker decided that she should take a job (workfare) at an agency that takes care of the needs of senior citizens. She worked there for some time, but couldn't make ends meet. She asked her welfare worker if she could find a training program, but the worker wants her to keep searching for other employment.

The disenfranchisement of Aboriginal women, be they "status," Métis, "Bill C-31's" or any other state-imposed category, has been consistent throughout the colonial period and into the present. While women are hurt the most by health and social problems, economic and political marginalization and the two-tiered justice system, we have the least say in naming the issues, identifying solutions or dialoging with government. The Aboriginal women within NAC believe that the Canadian government must move to fulfill the commitments made at the Beijing Fourth World Conference on Women.

While it is extremely regrettable that our communities have been divided and further subdivided according to Department of Indian Affairs and Northern Development (DIAND) membership criteria, this is the reality we face today. And while we cannot speak for all indigenous women, there are some common threads and concerns that can be drawn upon. With this in mind, the writer would like readers to know that she does have legal "status," a privilege that accrues rights and benefits not available to "non-status" and "non-treaty" women. Urban residency also affords similar experiences.

Poverty and Child Welfare

Aboriginal women are, statistically, "the poorest of the poor," both on- and off-Reserve. And while we lead the nation in elevated levels of unemployment and illiteracy, we lack the opportunities and support to move out of these disadvantaged positions.

Placing responsibility for deficit reduction, both federally and provincially, on the poor has worsened this situation for Aboriginal women. Mounting financial and social pressures often result in the supposed "voluntary" placement of children into the care of the Ministry of Social Services. For example, women, both on- and off-Reserve, applying for in-patient alcohol, drug and substance abuse treatment programs are forced to place their children into temporary care. And the new child welfare laws, which impose greater monitoring of women in many parts of the country, make the apprehension of Aboriginal children routine. The absence of on-Reserve childcare programs and services leaves mothers with few options. Governments insist upon attacking social programs, and yet support services that would prevent apprehension of children are precisely what is required by single mothers, particularly those in the cities who are most vulnerable to the authorities.

Housing

The exemption of on-Reserve communities from Provincial Property Laws and Labour Codes puts status Aboriginal women at a severe disadvantage. When family breakdowns occur, women and children are usually the ones forced to live off-Reserve. Similarly, when conflicts arise in band offices between male-dominated leadership and female-dominated support staff, power relations often leave Aboriginal women in compromised positions. That status Aboriginal women must leave the Reserve is borne out by the fact that the majority of off-Reserve status Indians are women. And off-Reserve residency results in these women being left out of the decision-making process on political and economic development and other critical issues within their homelands. Some of these women have been driven from their homelands and many others have never been allowed to return. The re-instatement of status through Bill C-31 has not meant recognition of entitlements belonging to these Aboriginal women and their children. Only a few of these women have been provided with on-Reserve housing, which would allow them to return home.

Violence against Aboriginal Women and the Justice System

The many disappearances and deaths of young Aboriginal women in the northern interior of British Columbia and the many women killed each year in east Vancouver emphasize how racism, sexism and poverty interact to make women vulnerable. A newspaper headline about another Aboriginal woman killed in Le Pas by another white man screams of the "two-tiered justice system," but it no longer has shock value. Reviews such as the Manitoba Aboriginal Justice Inquiry, the Caribou Justice Inquiry and the Royal Commission on the Donald Marshall case indicate the level of racism, sexism and classism within the justice system, yet these go unabated. The justice system fails Aboriginal women, women who are victims of violence and Aboriginal women who are incarcerated.

When Aboriginal women are incarcerated, there aren't the culturally appropriate healing programs and educational and other services that are available to Canadian women or Aboriginal men. The lack of representation of Aboriginal women in the creation of alternative justice models means that those most victimized by violence are excluded from meaningful decision-making processes. Healing lodges such as those in southern Saskatchewan have proven to be far more valuable than a prison cell. In addition to the need for advocacy and support services, greater involvement of Aboriginal women in the planning and delivery of justice systems for Aboriginal communities, both on- and off-Reserve, is critical.

Health and Social Development

Demographic data indicates that Aboriginal women are the frontline workers and service providers in our own communities. We address such health concerns as cervical and breast cancer, diabetes, AIDS, and fetal alcohol syndrome (FAS). We are the social development workers, counsellors and educators who address addictions, literacy, unemployment, wife battering, child abuse, child apprehension, teenage pregnancies and the needs of sex trade workers. Based upon these observations and upon lived experience, we assert the need for better access to quality healthcare services and to an adequate standard of living.

While there are some Aboriginal organizations that offer services addressing these same concerns, Aboriginal women have minimal amounts of power in identifying strategies or shaping the goals of such services. We believe that, since we feel the greatest impact of these social problems and are the professional staff who deliver these services, our input should be sought. As the keepers of the culture, we believe that we can revitalize our roles as teachers, midwives, mentors, mothers, grandmothers and aunts, roles which were stolen from us by the Residential School system, the missionaries, the Indian agents and the Indian Act.

Education

Education is one of the tools required for effective self-governance, as well as for understanding the larger society around us. With high school graduation levels for Aboriginal students being far below general Canadian norms, it makes no sense for DIAND to target postsecondary education for funding cuts. Despite protest by Aboriginal students and their communities, DIAND refuses to lift the "cap on funding."

Public education funding directed at Aboriginal students is virtually unavailable to "Bill C-31's" and other urban-based Aboriginal peoples. Additionally, Aboriginal women service providers require training opportunities to advance within their agencies and organizations. We need to move into positions that will allow greater autonomy and agency to affect the problems that plague us.

The Human Rights of Aboriginal Women

Because of the colonial governments' encouragement of patriarchy and their support of male leadership, Aboriginal women have been dealt out of positions of power. We would, once again, like to have full and equal participation. This means involvement in all future constitutional, self-government and treaty negotiations. In addition, we would like to see a gender analysis of the Indian Act conducted to bring our civil and political rights on par with "status" Aboriginal men and with Canadian women. Canadian women enjoy the protection of the Canadian Charter of Rights and Freedoms and the Canadian Human Rights Act that on-Reserve Aboriginal women do not. The federal government must recognize our right to self-governance, whether we live on our homelands or in the cities, but the human rights of Aboriginal women must also be protected.

Political and Economic Disenfranchisement

As defenders of Aboriginal rights and our claims to the land, we urge the federal government to live up to its fiduciary obligation of protecting our "special status," rather than striving to download legal and financial responsibilities onto provincial and municipal governments. From this position, we continue to demand our place within our homelands, amongst our families and communities. Further, we exhort

the federal government to recognize our right to self-governance, whether we live on our homelands or in the cities. We
would, for example, like to have the opportunity to express
our positions and perspectives on how DIAND spends child
welfare dollars "on our behalf." Since our names and numbers on Band Registries are used in DIAND funding formulas, we call for more equitable formulas for the distribution
of programs and services, especially postsecondary education funding.

We feel the greatest impact of colonization and truly
believe that we continue to live under neocolonial rule. Political and economic disenfranchisement of Aboriginal
women must come to an end. Pro-active measures must be
taken to ensure that Aboriginal women have the resources,
infrastructure and ongoing supports necessary to carry out
the organizing, consultations, education and research to end
our marginalization.

Questions:

1. Will your party include Aboriginal women in its consultations on changes or amendments to the Indian Act?

Liberal Party (Liberals)
> Liberal Minister for Indian Affairs and Northern
> Development Ron Irwin announced changes to the
> Indian Act without consultation.

Bloc Québécois
> Failed to respond.

Reform Party
> Failed to respond.

New Democratic Party (NDP)
> Existing NDP policy commits them to continue
> "lobbying on behalf of the Native women in Can-
> ada to ensure their equal representation, through

their national organizations, in all relevant deliberations concerning the rights of Aboriginal people in Canada, including Parliamentary Committees and meetings and conferences respecting the Canada Constitution Act and continues to call upon the Federal Government to provide the funding necessary to facilitate their full participation."

Progressive Conservative Party (Tories)
In regards to the Indian Act, the Tories state that "ineffective, paternalistic and colonial approaches of the Indian Act must give way to greater self-reliance, local control, and the eventual elimination of the Department of Indian Affairs and Northern Development (DIAND) and the Indian Act leading to self-government." They also state that Aboriginal people "must be equal partners in any discussions that affect their future ..." However, they fail to state how Aboriginal women would be integral to this discussion.

2. Will your party ensure the relevancy of such programs as justice, child welfare and anti-violence by actively seeking the involvement and input of Aboriginal women? (All quotes from Allan Rock of the Liberal Party are from "Consultation on Violence Against Women, June 13, 1996: A Report on the Recommendations made to the Minister of Justice Canada.")

Liberal Party (Liberals)
Minister of Justice Allan Rock has stated that the government is spending between $6 million and $7 million a year in about 25 to 30 Aboriginal reserve communities and in about 8 to 12 Aboriginal urban communities to create "different models for the administration of justice."
Rock himself acknowledges that this amount is "a relative pittance."

Rock states that "... it's a fundamental part of this approach that women would be involved in the organization of these approaches, of these communities and of their administration" and that "... none of the projects would be approved unless we were satisfied, unless women were satisfied that they had been fully involved in their preparation." He adds that "it's an integral part of the process that women are involved in the structuring of the committees, the determination of criteria, deciding what options would be available, when they would be exercised."

But, on the issue of providing stable funding to Aboriginal women's organizations to ensure their meaningful involvement in this process, Minister Rock was noncommittal.

Bloc Québécois
Failed to respond.

Reform Party
Failed to respond.

New Democratic Party (NDP)
The NDP state that "it is essential to consult with Aboriginal women in developing programs that are culturally relevant and serve their needs. It is especially important that Aboriginal women are consulted in the development of essential programs in the areas of justice, child welfare and anti-violence. The government has a responsibility to actively seek the input and involvement of Aboriginal women in designing these programs."

Progressive Conservative Party (Tories)
The Tories state that "Aboriginal self-government should aim to establish the conditions for improved self-reliance and self-esteem through effective edu-

cation, economic development and social justice."
However, they do not state that Aboriginal women
would be included in this process.

The following two questions did not receive sufficient response from enough federal parties to provide a comparison
of party positions. However, readers may want to ask these
questions when they are deciding who to vote for.

3. What will you do to ensure that Aboriginal women are
represented in land claims, self-government and constitutional and treaty negotiations with government?

4. Will you provide adequate funding for healthcare, housing
and education? Further, will you strive for greater accountability from Aboriginal governments for the equitable distribution of programs and services?

4

Immigration, Refugee and Migrant Workers' Policies

Nandita Sharma

———————————

Sharifa[1], who resides in Windsor, Ontario, is a single parent of three children. She has recently been granted convention refugee status. While she very much wants to work, she has been unable to find employment and must depend on social assistance benefits to support her family. When Sharifa and her family were finally granted refugee status, she began the process of applying for landed immigrant status. Little did she realize the actual cost of becoming a permanent resident in Canada. She scraped together the fee for the application: $500 for herself and two of her children and $500 for another over the age 18. Her expenses did not end at $1,000. Sharifa also had to pay the Head Tax, all together another $1,950! Sharifa approached her caseworker for assistance. When she received no help there, she reached out to her community and received a loan. She was honest and told her caseworker about the loan. One month later she received a letter from the Ministry of Community and Social Services informing her that over $65 would be deducted from her monthly mother's allowance until the sum of $1,950 was recovered. In effect the provincial government penalized

Sharifa for taking a loan to pay for the federal government's Head Tax. As a result, Sharifa must make do with a smaller monthly check plus pay $50 every month to the person who lent her the money. She must also provide for herself and three dependents. Another consequence of the Head Tax is that her eldest child will have to defer plans to attend community college. It is too expensive for someone not yet granted landed immigrant status.

Immigration policies help set the legal as well as social boundaries of who is seen as "belonging" in Canada and who isn't. Politicians who will not admit to being racists promote anti-immigrant or anti-multiculturalism policies and practices. Their complaints about "too many" immigrants started when more of our immigrants were people of colour. There were "too many" when they were from "Third World" countries. In reality, the proportion of immigrants to the Canadian-born population has not changed since 1951.

Politicians have blamed immigrants and refugees for unemployment and cutbacks in social programs. The rhetoric is that immigrants and refugees take away jobs from so-called "Canadians" and abuse the welfare system. We see this view reflected in newspaper articles like the one published on November 10, 1995, in *The Toronto Star* under the headline "Ottawa to crack down on immigrants' sponsors." The reality is much different from these racist attacks.

What we hear less often is that immigrants pay more in taxes than they ever receive in social services (see "Immigrants help economy, report says," *The Globe and Mail*, November 22, 1995). Immigration actually increases government revenue and creates a net tax benefit! Immigrants create jobs for people in Canada by using goods and services (such as housing, food, clothing, etc.). The government's own study, published in 1987, showed that between 1983 and 1985 immigrants and refugees created thousands of new jobs. It also indicated that immigrants and refugees are less likely to commit major crimes than the Canadian-born population.

The attacks against immigrants and refugees have been harmful to women. Over the last 25 years, women of colour have entered Canada mainly as sponsored immigrants and refugees. The right wing tell us that people who are sponsored (mostly women of colour and their children) do not contribute to the economy or that they are "non-productive." They say that these women and children should be restricted from entering the country.

Canada's use of a "point system" to select immigrants reproduces the sexist and racist segregation of Canada's labour market. The points system values only certain skills and training (usually that of men) and largely devalues the work that women have been responsible for, such as domestic work and sewing work. This system also makes it difficult or impossible for working-class people and people living in poverty to enter Canada. Demands made for certain types of education, language skills and training favour middle-class and wealthy male immigrants. The right wing want to expand these discriminatory criteria to anyone they deem "uneconomical."

These right-wing changes to immigration and refugee policy are happening all over the world. Across the globe, we see more closed borders and greater limits on the rights of immigrants and refugees. At the same time, governments are opening up their borders to transnational corporations. Trillions of dollars are moved around the world by the corporate owners. Corporations are given citizenship status (the right to national treatment) with corporations from either the US or Mexico treated the same as those from Canada. This is happening at a time when the automatic right of citizenship to children born in Canada to non-permanent residents is being threatened and when Canada is relying on a large labour force of migrant workers who are denied the same rights as others.

Liberals' Pre-election Promises: The Rhetoric

During the 1993 federal election campaign, Sergio Marchi, the Liberal's first minister of Citizenship and Immigration, promised that the Liberal Party would be a "friend" to refugees and immigrants.

A specific promise made in the Red Book was to have immigration levels set at 1 percent of the population of Canada. This would have meant approximately 300,000 new immigrants per year. The Liberals have not met this target. In 1996, about 205,000 immigrants will have moved to Canada. This rate means that one-third fewer immigrants were admitted in 1996 than the Liberals promised.

Most of the cuts have come from the family-class of immigration. This is the main avenue for women to be able to move to Canada. The Liberals reduced family-class immigration by over 20 percent. The Liberals now state that they will stay the same course, and in 1997 they will only admit between 195,000 and 220,000 immigrants and refugees. The new minister of Citizenship and Immigration, Lucienne Robillard, has said that the Liberals will not meet their Red Book promise because they recognize the scapegoating of immigrants and refugees that occurs. Instead of doing something concrete about debunking these harmful myths, the Liberal government has chosen to play into the hands of the bigots who repeat falsehoods against immigrants and refugees.

The Current Liberal Government's Record: The Reality

The policies followed by the Liberals in government have reflected a right-wing shift. The Liberal government has basically adopted the Reform Party's plan on immigration. In fact, Reform MP Art Hanger says that the Reform Party should take full credit for bringing the immigration debate to the House of Commons and that the party takes credit for moving the government's policies further to the right.

The imposition of a Head Tax on immigrants from China in the late nineteenth and early twentieth century is a shameful part of Canadian history. However, in February 1995 the Liberal government imposed its equivalent: a $975 Head Tax or "Right to Landing Fee" on all immigrants and refugees over the age of 19. This Head Tax was imposed through the Finance Ministry with the collusion of the Ministry of Citizenship and Immigration. The Head Tax must be paid before a person is able to become a landed immigrant in Canada. The Liberals stated that the Head Tax was intended to cover the costs of immigration services. Yet, the money raised by this tax (about $146 million a year) has not been used for this purpose. In fact, the Liberals have made cuts to settlement services, have reduced immigration department staff by 20 percent (over 1,000 workers) and have eliminated almost all labour-market training programs.

The Liberals stated that the Head Tax is not discriminatory since everyone over 19 has to pay it. Yet, it is clearly easier for the wealthy from the "First World" countries to pay this fee. The impact of the policy means that it does favour some over others.

The Liberals claim that their loan program assists low-income refugees and immigrants who can't pay the tax. Yet to get this loan, immigrants have to meet the same requirements they would if they were applying for a loan from a bank. This has stopped many people from receiving the loan.

In March 1997 the Liberals imposed discriminatory rules that, in effect, privatized social services for family-class immigrants. Now, these immigrants no longer have the same right to collect social assistance as others in Canada. Instead, the person sponsoring the new immigrant will be forced to pay for these social services out of pocket. This new rule ignores the fact that immigrants and those who sponsor them both pay taxes in Canada and should have equal access to social programs and services. Such a move further perpetrates the notion that immigrants, particularly family-class immigrants, are a "burden" to Canadian society when this is clearly untrue.

In a move to further stratify and polarize Canadian society, the Liberal government has proposed to eliminate the human right of automatic citizenship. The minister of Citizenship and Immigration has publicly stated the intent of the Liberals to consider a proposal to deny Canadian citizenship to some children born in Canada. Initially the government is looking at denying the children of refugee claimants citizenship status even if born in Canada. If a child born here is not considered to be Canadian, then who is safe from the government's threat to deny the rights of citizenship to any one of us in this country?

The Liberals continue the discriminatory labelling of immigrants with disabilities as a "burden" on the healthcare system and have denied them the chance to be reunited with their families in Canada.

Immigration recruitment schemes are placing more emphasis on the applicant's ability to speak English or French. Ability is judged by immigration officers, most of whom are white. Again, this puts more barriers in place for people coming from "Third World" countries.

The rights of refugees are under attack by the Liberal government. The Liberals have pushed very strongly for the "Safe Third Country" agreement with the US which would seriously undermine Canada's international human rights agreements to protect refugees fleeing persecution. Since their first year in government, the Liberals have cut the number of refugees admitted to Canada by 35 percent (from 44,000 to 28,000). Since then, they have denied refugees the right to appeal a negative decision made by the Immigration and Refugee Board (IRB) on the merits of their refugee claim. To make matters worse, the Liberals have introduced legislation that would leave only one person (instead of two) sitting on the panel of the IRB that determines whether someone gains refugee status or not.

Refugees to Canada fall into two categories: Convention Refugees and Designated Refugees. Convention Refugees are those who are recognized as refugees under the United Nations Convention on Refugees. Designated Refugees are those who are in refugee-like situations but do not meet the UN standards. Designated Refugees in Canada are unable to collect the food, clothing and housing allowance provided for resettlement. This division between refugees started under the previous Liberal government.

The Liberal government has proven to be inflexible and has ignored many public appeals to stay the deportation of women victims of male violence or those fleeing gender-related persecution. The Liberals have also failed to make the current "Women at Risk" program, a program that NAC and other groups fought for, meaningful, because the number of women admitted to Canada under its authority remains shockingly small.

Canada has further ignored international standards by reversing the practice of refusing to deport refugees to unsafe countries. Now refugees may be returned to unsafe countries. In 1990, only 3,039 people were deported. By 1994, there were 8,296 deportations.

Furthermore, persons with criminal convictions anywhere in the world and on any charge will no longer be considered for immigrant status. This policy applies to political prisoners. People with criminal records of any kind are no longer able to claim refugee status. Recently, several people from South Africa were denied entry into Canada because of the actions that they had taken to resist apartheid. The Department of Citizenship and Immigration labelled these past political prisoners as criminals.

The Liberal government has demanded DNA testing for people who are being sponsored by family members in Canada. The Liberals say that this expensive testing is being done to ensure that the sponsor is related to the person he/she is sponsoring. However, this policy is not being implemented across the board and seems to target people from "Third World" countries such as Bangladesh, Ghana, Haiti, Jamaica and Vietnam.

Many are surprised to learn that Canada has a "guest worker" program called the Non-Immigrant Employment Authorization Program (NIEAP). This program issues a yearly average of 200,000 temporary work permits to migrant workers in the primary, service and manufacturing sectors. In 1995, almost 59,000 of these temporary work permits were issued to women. Most of the people who are forced to work in this program as a condition of entering and staying in Canada work and live in substandard conditions. People admitted under the NIEAP are denied the same economic, social and political rights ensured to permanent residents and citizens. So, while corporations are given "citizenship rights" through the North American Free Trade Agreement, the government denies it to people who are recruited as cheap migrant workers in Canada.

Finally, Former Minister for Human Resources Development, Doug Young (now Defence), made the classic anti-immigrant comment to his colleague, Bloc Québécois MP Osvaldo Nunez, in response to a routine question in the House of Commons. Young said, "If you're not happy, get yourself another country." Such a profoundly undemocratic comment makes it clear that the Liberals believe that any questions about Liberal policy from immigrants (or people believed to be immigrants — Nunez is a Canadian citizen) should be met with scorn and racism.

To sum it all up, it is clear that despite numerous studies and government reports that show the positive contributions of immigrants and refugees, the Liberals have continued to impose restrictive regulations and lower immigration targets. NAC believes that the Liberals have used the area of immigration and refugee policy to divert peoples' attention away from their failed economic and social policies through scapegoating tactics.

Questions:

1. Where do the parties stand on increasing, decreasing or maintaining the number of sponsored immigrants currently admitted under the family-class?

Liberal Party (Liberals)
> The Liberals' record shows that they are in favour of decreasing the number of immigrants admitted under the family-class. They have already cut family-class sponsorship by 20 percent.

Bloc Québécois (Bloc)

The Bloc state they would maintain the current levels of immigration (below 1 percent of the population).

The Bloc, however, are "worried" about the lower level of immigrants admitted under the family-class and would likely give greater priority to family-class immigration over so-called "independent" immigrants.

Reform Party (Reform)

The Reform Party favours decreasing the number of immigrants admitted under the family-class.

Reform have run on a platform promising stricter admission criteria and cuts in the family-class category.

New Democratic Party (NDP)

The NDP favour increasing family-class immigration and believe that family reunification should be the centrepiece of Canada's immigration policy.

The NDP would increase overall immigration levels to up to 1 percent of the Canadian population.

The NDP would give greater priority to family-class immigration over so-called "independent" immigrants.

Progressive Conservative Party (Tories)

The Tories state that there have not been enough "economic immigrants" in recent years, meaning that there have been "too many" family-class immigrants.

In their policy statements, the Tories state that there must be "more emphasis on the selection of immigrants with the skill, education and language abilities needed by Canada."

The Tories cite so-called "experts" who say that "recent immigrants have not done as well economically as previous generations of newcomers and that we do not have the resources to deal with the pressures placed upon our social infrastructure by large numbers of immigrants who lack facility in at least one of the official languages."

2. Currently, those who wish to sponsor family members for the purpose of family reunification are the only ones in Canada who are legally obliged to support those they sponsor regardless of job loss, sickness or other reasons making financial support impossible. It must be remembered that those who sponsor new immigrants, as well as new immigrants themselves, contribute more in tax dollars than they ever receive in public services.

Where do the parties stand on favouring the elimination of the requirement to sign an undertaking of financial commitment when sponsoring family members to Canada?

Liberal Party (Liberals)
>The Liberals' record shows that they do not favour eliminating the requirement to sign an undertaking of financial commitment but favour increasing the penalties against sponsors who (often through no fault of their own) are unable to financially support those they sponsor.

Bloc Québécois (Bloc)
>The Bloc favour the elimination of the requirement of financial commitment when sponsoring spouses or children.
>The Bloc would have decisions regarding sponsorship and criteria for admitting immigrants fall under exclusive Quebec jurisdiction.

Reform Party (Reform)
>Reform do not favour eliminating the requirement to sign an undertaking of financial commitment.

Reform are in favour of eliminating the right of sponsored immigrants to access social programs if their sponsors are unable to meet their needs and believe that the sponsors should cover all financial requirements, regardless of their ability to do so. Reform, therefore, are in favour of a two-tier system of access to social programs with sponsored immigrants being denied this access.

New Democratic Party (NDP)
The NDP do not favour eliminating the requirement to sign an undertaking of financial commitment.

The NDP state that the requirement to sign such an undertaking should be "well balanced" with the humanitarian and family reunification goals of immigration policy.

Progressive Conservative Party (Tories)
The Tories state that "... we do not have the resources to deal with the pressures placed upon our social infrastructure by large numbers of immigrants who lack facility in at least one of the official languages." They do not specifically state a position on the question.

3. Currently, the Canadian government uses a very limited definition of "family" in its family-class sponsorship program by recognizing only a nuclear, heterosexual family model. Where do the parties stand on favouring the expansion of the definition of family to include culturally diverse definitions of family as well as lesbian and gay families?

Liberal Party (Liberals)
The Liberals do not favour a non-discriminatory definition of family that includes culturally diverse definitions of family as well as lesbian and gay families.

At best, the Liberals discuss the possibility of using their discretionary powers and taking a person-by-person approach to what are, fundamentally, human rights issues. They state that they "might process individuals" who are excluded in the definition of family currently provided in the Immigration Act through humanitarian and compassionate grounds.

Bloc Québécois (Bloc)
The Bloc "do not have a position" on this issue at this time.

Reform Party (Reform)
The Reform Party does not favour expanding the definition of family to include culturally diverse definitions of family as well as lesbian and gay families.

Reform believe that only spouses of the opposite sex, minor dependent children and aged dependent parents should be admitted under the family-class.

New Democratic Party (NDP)
The NDP believe in expanding the definition of family to include lesbian and gay families. However, the NDP have not publicly committed to allowing for culturally diverse definitions of family.

The NDP say that "all close family members including all children" should be admitted under the family-class. They are not specific on how restrictive or expansive their understanding of "close" family members is.

Progressive Conservative Party (Tories)
Failed to respond.

4. The Liberal government is currently considering eliminating the automatic right of citizenship to children born in

Canada if the parents do not have landed status in the country (for example, if the parents are refugees). Where do the parties stand on the elimination of the automatic right of citizenship to children born in the country regardless of the immigration or citizenship status of the parents?

Liberal Party (Liberals)
In early 1996, the Liberal Minister of Citizenship and Immigration Lucienne Robillard stated that the Liberal government is considering eliminating the automatic right to Canadian citizenship.

In October 1996, as the Liberal election campaign began, the same minister stated that she was going to consider the matter some time "next year" (post-election?) and that more studies needed to be done on the matter.

Bloc Québécois (Bloc)
The Bloc are opposed to eliminating the automatic right of citizenship.

Reform Party (Reform)
The Reform Party is in favour of eliminating the automatic right to Canadian citizenship.

In addition, a Reform government would move responsibility for immigration to Foreign Affairs and the Department of Justice, creating the potential of further criminalizing immigrants and refugees.

New Democratic Party (NDP)
The NDP are opposed to eliminating the automatic right of citizenship.

The NDP state that they "see no reason for the government to meddle with the citizenship of those born in Canada."

Progressive Conservative Party (Tories)
> It appears that the Tories agree with the removal of the automatic right of citizenship.
> They state that "the ability of refugees to gain Canadian citizenship as well as our generous social programs have led some observers to question whether some refugee claimants are 'asylum shopping'; that is, leaving a safe situation and coming to Canada as a matter of personal choice."

5. In February 1995, the Liberal government introduced a $975 Head Tax called the Right to Landing Fee. Everyone (immigrant or refugee) who wishes to be a permanent resident in Canada is required to pay it. The Head Tax makes it especially difficult for women, who control only 1 percent of the world's wealth, to enter or remain in Canada as permanent residents. The Head Tax represents an often insurmountable barrier to women entering through the family sponsorship program and has made the goal of family reunification an unattainable dream for many. As of October 1996, it cost a family of four a total of $3,150 (Canadian) to immigrate to Canada. For working-class families, for refugees fleeing persecution and for those living in countries with low foreign exchange rates to the Canadian dollar (mainly "Third World" countries), the Head Tax is an onerous burden.

Where do the parties stand on the Head Tax?

Liberal Party (Liberals)
> The Liberals favour the Head Tax. After all, it was the Liberals who made the historic move to bring it in. Since then, even after repeated calls for its repeal, they have not indicated that they intend to remove it. Canada is the only country in the world to charge a Head Tax to refugees.
> At the 1996 Liberal Party Policy Convention, however, a resolution was passed which committed the Party to "re-examine" the Head Tax to deter-

mine if it is warranted. The resolution allows the Liberals an option. It states that if the Head Tax is not abolished, it should be payable only after the arrival of the new immigrant in Canada.

Bloc Québécois (Bloc)
The Bloc are opposed to the imposition of the federal $975 Head Tax upon immigrants and refugees.

However, it appears that the Bloc's objection is not a principled one but one based on their belief that Quebec has jurisdiction over immigration policy.

Reform Party (Reform)
The Reform Party favours the Head Tax.

New Democratic Party (NDP)
The NDP are opposed to the Head Tax and recognize that it discriminates against poorer immigrants and refugees.

Progressive Conservative Party
Failed to respond.

Endnotes

1. "Sharifa" is a pseudonym.

5

Women with Disabilities

Indra Beharrysingh and Meenu Sikand

My name is Indra Beharrysingh and I have lived with a disability for 19 years. I am studying Bioethics at the University of Toronto and I hope to graduate this year. I have been blessed with the most supportive family and friends and I never give up no matter how daunting the road ahead might look. I was never treated differently by the people who mattered to me and so I came to perceive myself as no less important and integral to society as anybody else. My mother and father and my brother have always encouraged me to be all I can be and fulfill my dreams. I have also been blessed with the most special husband in the world. I have always known that even though I may have special needs there is more to me and to life than the issue of whether or not I walk. I am equal in my humanity. Life is a learning experience filled with many splendors and I look forward to the enrichment that life's little idiosyncrasies bring to me. Yet, there persists at various levels of society obstacles that prevent access to resources that are essential to the economic independence and well-being of women with disabilities. These resources should be available to all. As I approach the end of my current academic pursuits the reality that I face is wrought with uncertainty and increasing negative initiatives from our government(s) (at various levels). Their refusal to assume responsibility of a leadership role translates into rising unemployment for women with disabilities, increased poverty, diminished quality of health care, reduction of vital transportation services, cancellation of employment equity ... the list seems endless and it is growing all of the time. This lack of commitment from those whom we entrust to ensure the protection of our general well-being results in mounting fears and harsh realities for many women with disabilities. Women with disabilities can no longer be ignored as a supposedly unproductive, unambitious segment of society who must be treated with pity and condescension. Our endeavor for independence and equality of opportunity is by no means past, but it is now shared by a united, mighty voice — that of Canadian women with disabilities. Ours is not a struggle in vain. We will overcome.

According to the World Health Organization, disability may be defined as a physical or mental, visible or invisible condition that results in restriction or lack (resulting from an impairment) of ability to perform an activity in the manner within the range considered normal.

The Disability Rights Committee of NAC act as advocates in the areas of healthcare, housing, the establishment of a Canadians with Disabilities Act and the appointment of a Secretary of State for Disability Issues, Canada Pension Plan (CPP), income tax, immigration and Vocational Rehabilitation of Disabled Persons (VRDP).

In Canada women with disabilities make up about 18 percent of the female population. Yet, discriminatory policies and the failure to fund services adequately combined with unequal access to resources prevent women with disabilities from enjoying their full citizenship rights in Canada. The rights to a good quality of life that Canadians are guaranteed under the Canadian Charter of Rights and Freedoms do not extend to women with disabilities equally because they cannot access these rights or because they are denied full opportunity to utilize these rights. Women with disabilities experience a double disadvantage under a patriarchal realm, occupying a lower socioeconomic status than disabled men and non-disabled women. This translates into poverty, loss of autonomy and loss of self-esteem. Women with disabilities are at the bottom of the disadvantaged heap.

In 1993 in an article in *Abilities*, a magazine for persons with disabilities, Prime Minister Jean Chrétien stated that he and his newly elected government wished to restore public trust. The Liberal Party would implement a plan of economic, social and political renewal by building a socioeconomic framework whereby all Canadians could pursue their individual and collective well-being. The Prime Minister acknowledged and reiterated the alarmingly high rate of unemployment for Canadians with disabilities, noting that it was worse still for women with disabilities.

The Liberal Party vowed to work to eliminate barriers that prevent independence and to establish strategies that promote it. Furthermore, the Liberal Party stated that it was committed to "turn the principles of equality into action for the benefit of *all* Canadians." It pledged efforts and support to ensure this, yet little has actually been done.

A Task Force on Disability Issues — "Equal Citizenship for Canadians with Disabilities: The Will to Act" — was established to address the concerns of persons with disabilities, including women. The Council of Canadians with Disabilities (CCD) recently gave the Task Force Report a "thumbs up." Some of the recommendations made in the report are

- building disability considerations into mainstream policies;

- presenting information regarding disability, related spending and all social spending including Canada Health and Social Transfer;

- setting aside funds for relevant programs to promote accessibility;

- putting in place a policy and program infrastructure to support and encourage social policy research and development ... projects that build on the work of this Task Force in all areas including citizenship, development, income support, the cost of disability and legislative reform.

The Task Force provides some answers to the questions of women with disabilities based on its content. These are very promising recommendations, yet until and unless they are implemented, women with disabilities will continue to find themselves in dire straits. The Task Force recommendations will, if implemented, eliminate some of the inherent barriers in our political and social system and promote employment, participation in our community and independence.

It should be noted, however, that the Task Force was appointed late in the Liberal Party's mandate — less than a year ago. No matter what the Liberal Party seems to be pledging or recommending, its actions are not reflecting or supporting these proposals. The proposals of the Task Force as they relate to our questions are as follows:

1. On the issue of the creation of a Secretary of State for Disability Issues and a Canadians with Disabilities Act, the Task Force recognizes these needs and recommends the establishment of both.

2. On the issue of a Vocational Rehabilitation of Disabled Persons Act, the Task Force has strongly recommended that the current $168 million program continue and focus on an "Employability Program Access Fund," which would primarily support individuals with disabilities to become and remain employed.

3. On the issue of income tax, the Task Force has made several recommendations to improve recognition of disability-related costs, including the development of a new refundable Disability Expense Tax Credit and recognition of family care-giving, which is done primarily by women.

4. On the issue of the Immigration Act, section 19, as it affects persons with disabilities, the Act was amended and

specific reference to "disability" was removed. There remains, however, the exclusion of persons who will create
"excessive demand" on health and community services. This
amendment would define excessive demand as any condition
that would surpass that of the average non-disabled Canadian
over the age of 5. In essence, persons with disabilities are
still discriminated against by the Act.

5. On the issue of housing, the federal government appears
to be transferring the responsibility of more and more basic
needs and concerns to the provinces, who in turn relegate
them to the municipal governments. This is tantamount to
the federal government abdicating its responsibility.

6. On the issue of healthcare, this is another area where
the federal government seems to be relegating more responsibility to the provinces. While the federal government pays
lip service to the idea of protecting the "high" standard of
healthcare in Canada and ensuring that quality service is
available to all Canadians, regardless of their social status or
financial situation, its cutting actions do not seem to support
such sentiments.

7. On the issue of the CPP, the Government Consultation
Paper for 1996 proposed cuts, but because of federal and
provincial discord no action has been taken.

Immigration

Canada currently excludes persons with disabilities from
immigrating because they are considered "an excessive demand on health and social services." Although the Immigration Act was amended to remove a specific reference to
"disability," if section 19 is proclaimed and enforced, it will
allow for exclusion based on illness, disease, or a condition
that, in the government's eyes, will create an "excessive
demand." In addition, the government is creating new regulations to add to the Act that would include defining "excessive
demand" as any condition exceeding that of the average Canadian over the age of 5 who is not disabled.

Consultation, particularly with the immigrant community
and disability groups, has not been sought on these matters, yet

the consequences of these proposals will have dire and lasting effects on persons with disabilities and their families who wish to immigrate to Canada. This issue was not fully addressed by the Task Force. Families will be forced to discriminate against their kin because of disability. Furthermore, this will encourage Canadians to discriminate against Canadians with disabilities.

Women, as the primary caregivers, will be directly affected by new amendments to the Immigration Act. Families will be broken up, leaving women behind to care for disabled members of the family. These regulations violate the equality rights of persons with disabilities and their families under the Canadian Charter of Rights and Freedoms. With their narrow focus on monetary concerns, they eliminate the rights for persons with disabilities by assuming they have nothing of value to contribute to society.

Canadians with Disabilities Act and a Secretary of State for Disability Issues

Canadians with disabilities have the right to be full and equal participants in their communities. These fundamental rights are not subject to exclusion based on physical or mental, visible or invisible disabilities. The implementation, enforcement and monitoring of these rights are the responsibility and prerogative of the Canadian government as they are guaranteed under the Canadian Charter of Rights and Freedoms. They cannot be the sole responsibility of provincial or municipal governments.

There is a definite need for the federal government to create a Canadians with Disabilities Act and to appoint a Secretary of State for Disability Issues to ensure and protect the rights and interests of Canadians with disabilities in an equitable manner. The federal government should play a leadership role in urging the provinces to develop a common approach.

Vocational Rehabilitation of Disabled Persons Act

The VRDP is a $168 million program to cost-share vocational rehabilitation with the provinces. The Canadian government, however, has refused so far to make a commitment to continue the VRDP. The Federal Task Force on Disability Issues has strongly recommended continuing funding for VRDP, but that it be refocused as an "Employability Program Access Fund." The EPAF would primarily support *individuals* with disabilities in becoming employed and provide support and resources to help people with disabilities remain employed. It would have a partnerships and innovations component as well.

Employment programs are more cost effective because employed people pay taxes, spend more in the economy and are less dependent on public programs. Most important of all, increased employment opportunities ensure that people with disabilities can participate more fully in society. We recommend that the cost of this initiative be shared by the federal and provincial governments to cover all adults with disabilities, regardless of their income or employment status.

Canada and Quebec Pension Plan

The Canada and Quebec Pension Plan is currently under public attack, particularly the disability pension component of the plan. The CPP/QPP is extremely important to women and to persons with disabilities because it is accessible to all (including those with low incomes), it is portable, and its coverage is continued during temporary absences from the workforce due to childcare responsibilities or disability. For all these reasons, Canadian women with disabilities need a strong CPP/QPP. In fact, the CPP/QPP should be expanded to provide coverage to all women who are caregivers for children or for family members with disabilities (currently, the "childbearing dropout" applies only where the child is under 7).

Income Tax Issues

The Income Tax System should treat people with disabilities fairly by recognizing both the direct expenses and the indirect costs of disabilities. The current system fails to do this. The current definition of "disability" is so narrow that it denies the Disability Tax Credit to many who should get it. Many disability related costs — for attendant care, for moving expenses, for work-related supports, for nutritional supplements or for family care-giving — are recognized only to a very limited extent or not at all. Also, the Disability Tax Credit and Medical Expense Credit are non-refundable, so low-income Canadians, including most women with disabilities, don't benefit from them.

The Federal Task Force on Disability Issues has recently made significant proposals to improve the recognition of disability-related costs in the tax system, including development of a new *refundable* Disability Expense Tax Credit, and recognition of family care-giving, which is primarily provided by women.

Healthcare

People with disabilities need equal access to healthcare services and guarantees that healthcare reform initiatives will not discriminate against persons with disabilities. The Canada Health Act sets national standards requiring provinces to provide universal access to health services. However, public healthcare is under attack and the definition of what those services are differs from province to province, so that services available in one province may not be available in another.

Many health services needed by persons with disabilities, including drugs and some long-term care services, are not routinely included under the Canada Health Act, creating an economic burden on persons with disabilities. New healthcare reform efforts are talking about restricting services to save costs by redefining what is medically necessary. This may discriminate against persons with disabilities if the definitions include only those services that will "cure" people. The federal government must continue to play a strong leadership role in establishing national standards and should review existing healthcare plans to ensure that they are in compliance with the Canada Health Act and that they do not discriminate against persons with disabilities, as guaranteed in the Canadian Charter of Rights and Freedoms.

Housing

People with disabilities want to live in their own homes or apartments in the community, but many cannot afford the necessary renovations. A special fund to pay for renovations is needed. It would also benefit seniors by allowing them to age at home. Renovation subsidies will save money by allowing people to live independently and take care of themselves rather than relying on more expensive government programs and supports.

Questions:

The Disability Rights committee of NAC sent out a list of questions to the Liberal Party, the Reform Party, the Bloc Québécois, the Progressive Conservative Party and the New Democratic Party. These questions were sent by e-mail and by fax. The parties were given more than a month to reply and were sent a follow-up urging a response. Only the New Democrats chose to furnish us with responses to the questions posed by concerned women with disabilities.

The Liberal Party ignored the questions, as did the Reform Party and the Bloc Québécois. The Conservative Party replied by saying that it does not have a platform and until it does it cannot (will not) address the issues of women with disabilities. Yet, these parties expect the vote of disabled women in Canada; or are we not an important voting segment of the Canadian constituency? The decision of four federal parties to disregard our efforts to elicit a response to these questions would appear to reflect an attitude of dangerous indifference. As a result of this poor response, we have included the questions put to the parties without the usual table format of responses, with the exception of question number 9, to which we received three party responses. We urge women to continue to pose these questions in All Candidates' Meetings and in other forums.

1. Does your party support the establishment of a Canadians with Disabilities Act and the appointment of a Secretary of State for Disability Issues?
2. Is your party committed to maintaining funding for the VRDP program at its current levels?
3. Does your party support the EPAF proposal made by the Federal Task Force on Disability Issues?
4. Is your party opposed to limiting or cutting back the CPP/QPP, especially the disability component?
5. Will your party support CPP/QPP coverage for all caregivers?
6. Is your party in support of and committed to implementing the income tax proposals made by the Task Force? Does it support any additional or differing proposals?
7. What will your government do to ensure that healthcare services and access to those services by persons with disabilities are maintained or expanded? What will you do to ensure that persons with disabilities are not discriminated against by provincial healthcare reform initiatives?
8. Does your party support returning full funding to renovation subsidy programs?
9. Where does your party stand on opposing the discrimination that people with disabilities encounter when trying to enter Canada as landed immigrants or as refugees?

Liberal Party (Liberals)
> The Liberals' record shows that they intend to continue to discriminate against people with disabilities by keeping in place medical admissibility requirements that disquality many people from entering Canada as landed immigrants or refugees.

Bloc Québécois (Bloc)
> The Bloc would not answer question #9 directly.

Reform Party (Reform)
> The Reform Party would continue the discrimination experienced by people with disabilities when

trying to enter Canada as permanent residents by keeping in place medical admissibility requirements.

New Democratic Party (NDP)
The NDP would end the discrimination faced by people with disabilities by eliminating the sweeping clause that insists that people with disabilities be able to support themselves without recourse to any public assistance.

Progressive Conservative Party
Failed to respond.

6

Lesbian Rights

Lesbian Issues Committee

Lesbians continue to be discriminated against in Canada. Lesbians with disabilities, lesbians of colour and Aboriginal lesbians face particular social and economic pressures due to ableism, racism and colonialism. To differing degrees, lesbians have been tolerated by society on the condition that we kept our lesbianism "in the closet." But lesbians reject this silencing. Like other oppressed groups, we want dignity and respect.

Lesbians have made some considerable gains since the formation of the first lesbian and gay rights organization in Vancouver in 1964. In 1969, homosexual acts were decriminalized in Canada. In 1977, Quebec was the first province to prohibit discrimination on the basis of sexual orientation. In 1979, the Canadian Human Rights Commission recommended that the federal government amend the Canadian Human Rights Act to identify sexual orientation as a ground for discrimination. But the federal government took a long time to act. The Canadian Charter of Rights and Freedoms became part of the Constitution in 1982 and in 1985, section 15, dealing with equality rights, came into effect. Section 15 encouraged an open-ended interpretation of discrimination, including, though not naming, sexual orientation. It was not until 1996, when the Chrétien government finally passed the amendment to the Canadian Human Rights Act, that it became explicit that discrimination on the basis of sexual orientation was illegal in Canada. The governments of Alberta, Northwest Territories, Prince Edward Island and Newfoundland and Labrador still have not amended their Human Rights legislation to include sexual orientation.

The extension of human rights coverage to lesbians is one step towards equality. However, some provinces have left language in the legislation that defines "spouse" as a partner of the opposite sex, and others have exempted employee benefits plans from the legislation. What's worse, there are still more than 50 federal statutes that limit spousal benefits and rights to partners of the opposite sex. A key example is the federal Income Tax Act, which does not permit the registration of pension plans that extend benefits to same-sex spouses.

As Cynthia Peterson and John Fisher of Equality for Gays and Lesbians Everywhere (EGALE) point out in "EGALE Backgrounder on Discrimination against Lesbians and Gays" (1996):

> These statutes marginalize the individual partners in same sex relationships, stigmatize their children, and undermine the effective functioning of their family units (e.g., by refusing to recognize the relationship between children and their de facto lesbian and gay parents for the purposes of succession, by refusing to permit lesbians and gay men to sponsor their foreign-born partners for the purposes of immigration, etc).

The recognition of same-sex couples as families is the fundamental equality issue for lesbians and gays today. Equality for same-sex couples means that lesbians and gay men are recognized as having partnerships that are as legitimate as those of heterosexuals. This interpretation of family challenges stereotypes of lesbians and gay men as sexually deviant and promiscuous. Sexuality is no longer a matter that can be closeted in the realm of the "private." Nor does it define everything lesbians are or do. But it does define us legally in Canada. All discriminatory legislation and regulations must be changed to grant lesbians, gay men and bisexuals equality as same-sex couples.

Many victories have been won by lesbians and gay men through court challenges. These decisions have involved guardianship rights for a disabled partner, survivors' rights to public housing, Medicare coverage to a partner, survivors' benefits under the Workers' Compensation Board of British Columbia, just cause for resigning from a job and relocating under Unemployment Insurance legislation. Unions have won same-sex spousal benefits such as dental and extended healthcare, and family and bereavement leave. A Board of Inquiry of the Ontario Human Rights Commission ordered the Ontario government to provide same-sex couples the same pension benefits as heterosexual couples. The Board ordered that all references to "opposite sex" be deleted from the definition of marital status in the Ontario Human Rights Code.

Some changes have been made to Canadian immigration procedures as a result of challenges by lesbian and gays. Lesbian and gays who apply to immigrate to Canada can be considered on humanitarian and compassionate grounds because of their same-sex partnership with a Canadian citizen or landed immigrant. However, they do not qualify for sponsorship under the family-class provisions, which also exclude culturally diverse definitions of family. In terms of refugees, lesbians may now qualify as refugees to Canada if they can prove they would be persecuted in their home country due to their sexual orientation. Despite these changes, some lesbians have been denied refugee status even though they presented strong proof that they would be persecuted.

Blatant discrimination against lesbians continues when they are denied access, custody or adoption on the basis of their sexual orientation. During this decade, the courts have tended towards considering lesbians as "suitable" parents, and several American states specifically permit adoption by same-sex couples. In other countries, same-sex couples have gained equal rights in all areas except adoption. Lesbians in

North America have won important decisions regarding their right to artificial insemination. Legal recognition does not mean that discriminatory behaviour will immediately change. Steps must be taken to protect lesbians against violence, which can range from verbal harassment to deadly assaults. Education programs, such as the "rainbow curriculum" in New York City schools, can address violence against people of colour, Aboriginal peoples, people with disabilities and lesbian and gay youth. Judges and the police must also be educated on these issues.

Liberal Record

The Liberals, and the Tories before them, took a long time to act on lesbian and gay rights. Finally, in 1996, the Liberal Bill C-33 was passed, amending the Canadian Human Rights Act (CHRA) to explicitly prohibit discrimination on the basis of sexual orientation. And it went further to extend health, dental, family and bereavement benefits to federal employees in same-sex relationships. However, C-33 did not address issues of marriage or adoption. In October 1996, the Prime Minister remarked that he was not "personally very comfortable" with same-sex marriage because "I don't know how that works in a society." This is a shocking comment from a leader who should know that same-sex marriages are legal in many Scandinavian countries.

The Liberal government is also credited with passage of Bill C-41. This amended the Criminal Code, providing for more severe penalties for crimes motivated by hatred on certain grounds, including race, religion, ethnicity, gender and sexual orientation.

Even though the Liberal government did amend the CHRA to include sexual orientation as a source of discrimination, these amendments do not ensure equality for lesbians under all federal legislation. For example the CHRA does not cover the equality rights of lesbians under the Income Tax Act and the Pension Benefits Standards Act. In order to guarantee full and equal rights for lesbians and gay men in Canada, the government must also explicitly recognize same-sex couples as families.

Question:

Will your party support the full recognition of same-sex couples as families, granting them the rights, benefits and freedoms that are accorded to heterosexual couples?

Liberal Party (Liberals)

The Liberals *do not support* the full recognition of same-sex couples as families by granting them the rights, benefits and freedoms that are accorded to heterosexual couples. They have refused to make amendments to the Income Tax Act and the Pension Benefits Standards Act to include coverage for same-sex couples.

While the Liberals brought in Bill C-33 (an act to include sexual orientation as a prohibited ground of discrimination in the CHRA), they are currently in court fighting a Charter challenge to win same-sex rights and benefits. Moreover, in October 1996, Prime Minister Jean Chrétien stated that he believes the definition of a married couple should be reserved for heterosexuals alone. (*Toronto Star*, October 17, 1996. "Chrétien rejects idea of gay marriage.")

Bloc Québécois

Failed to respond.

Reform Party (Reform)

The Reform Party *opposes* the full recognition of same-sex couples as families. Reform believe that "being married means being married to a person of the opposite sex."

Reform also believe that "marital status means the status of heterosexual couples" only and that "family status means the status of heterosexual couples and their natural or adopted issue."

Reform proposed an amendment to Bill C-33 (which allowed for the inclusion of sexual orientation as a prohibited ground of discrimination in the CHRA) that would have nullified the intent of this legislation. Reform wanted to add the following statement: "... the Government recognizes and affirms the importance of the traditional, heterosexual institution of marriage and family as the foundation of Canadian society and that nothing in this Act alters its fundamental role in society."

New Democratic Party (NDP)
They state: "Yes, [we] have advocated for a more inclusive definition of family to include gay and lesbian families. [Our] party policy advocates a definition that will clearly recognize that the relationships of lesbian and gay partners are equal and equivalent to the relationships of heterosexual spouses, in all matters under federal jurisdiction."

Progressive Conservative Party
Failed to respond.

7

Male Violence against Women

Male Violence against Women Committee

Andrea has had extensive contact with government systems to help deal with the abuse of her and her daughter by her husband. She states: Every day I hear about another government cut and I feel the impact immediately. I feel as if my place has been delegated to "rock bottom" for all times. My abusive and controlling ex-husband seems to be in total control of all our lives. Because of government changes, we cannot any longer get access to social service support; they keep telling us he will support us, but he doesn't. The Family Support Plan is a joke and puts a different spin on "your check is in the mail"!

My daughter ended up having to move in with her father, because he is "more financially secure." He is now sexually abusing her. Where is the justice? How can I look at myself, feeling impotent to care for her, keep her safe, when he and the government seem to be working together to keep us down!

"A state which tolerates violence against women within families or communities and which does not take effective measures to prevent this violence or hold accountable those who are responsible for the violence are as guilty as the individual perpetrators."

UN Special Rapporteur on
Violence Against Women

Statistics Canada in 1993 more than confirmed the statements of the Canadian women's movement: the government-commissioned survey found that over half the 12,000 women interviewed had been sexually or otherwise physically assaulted after the age of 16. They did not count childhood assaults.

International understandings and those developed in this country build on the knowledge that the solutions to violence against women lie in social development. The way to end most of the violence is to raise women in status. We must be equal to men, in everything, from pay checks to parenting, from education to pension rights, from the protection of laws to the protection from law.

The Canadian Charter of Rights and Freedoms promises us that equality. No government is free to ignore that law. Still the federal government is refusing to do what is necessary to establish that equal status for women.

Equality Reduces Violence

Women's groups have repeated the motto "equality reduces violence" since we invented transition houses and rape crisis centres in Canada in 1973.

Current governments choose between dealing with violence against women as an issue of equality or dealing with it only as an issue of criminal law and law enforcement. Confining the government initiatives to legal ones can make us dependent on law and order instead of positive social change. Promoting law and order has sometimes won elections, but it doesn't reduce violence against women. It is only the media name for a government program of more police with more guns, longer jail sentences and fewer civil liberties for everyone. Law and order doesn't reduce sexist violence. It doesn't even punish more men who commit violence against women.

Women want improvements in the justice system. For instance, we have demanded a faster and more effective response from the police to calls from women facing immediate violence. The federal government is directly responsible for RCMP policing that affects many women across the country. Of the 7,000 police in British Columbia for instance, 4,000 are RCMP members. Federal leadership and federal funds can affect many police practices. The most common complaint of women facing violence is that they cannot count on the police. Yet the Solicitor General has refused to consult with women's groups to improve the situation.

Women complained that husbands get away with stalking. Police claimed they needed a new law and, in spite of the opinion of feminists, the Liberals brought in the Stalking or Criminal Harassment Law. According to the government study just released, men, especially ex-husbands, continue to get away with stalking without police interference. We want the police to do an adequate investigation according to law and to get the results promptly to a prosecutor.

Prosecutors must be funded and directed to take the time necessary to assure criminal convictions and not to divert, plead down or otherwise bury these cases. We want these matters decided according to law and justice. We insist on the protection and promotion not only of the Charter rights of the accused but also of the Charter rights of women victims, witnesses and complainants. Instead, the Liberal government has increased the diversion from conviction, increased conditional sentencing and increased mediation rather than prosecution in cases of violence against women. One Ottawa prosecutor bragged on national television that he uses volunteers to mediate rape cases. The federal government policies promote mediation instead of criminal convictions of abusive husbands and fathers. The Access to Justice Internet Site even promotes fathers' rights groups with propaganda paid for by Canadian citizens.

Most of all, government should choose to deal with violent crimes as a problem of social development. To do so would lead to funding equality seeking women's groups, providing them with money and other resources to design policies that improve women's place in society. We don't want victims' rights; we want the rights that can prevent us from being victimized. Besides being just, this new status for women will reduce women's vulnerability to attacks.

Instead, the policies introduced by the Liberals have further undermined the general status of women. These are not separate issues. For example, they repealed the Canada Assistance Plan. Without a right to welfare across the country, how does a woman who is beaten and unemployed leave her abusive husband? Even if she can manage a job later, during the transition period she is likely to need welfare. In Canada in 1997 she may not get it. The government has left it up to each province to decide. This, just when the federal government gave each province less to spend on such social services. Even if the woman has a job, her need for a transition house, childcare program, education or language training can still sabotage her flight to freedom.

In "Locked in and Left Out," a survey by the Ontario Association of Interval and Transition Houses (OAITH) that was released in November 1996, women surveyed by transition houses have said that the reduction in social services forced 66 percent of women to remain with abusive partners. In the same survey, 50 percent of the shelters reported that women now saw shelters as temporary escapes rather than as a beginning.

Frontline workers know that the promotion of women' equality reduces the trend to violence. In 1993 NAC published "99 Steps Toward an End to Violence Against Women." This document compiled the facts, analysis and proposals for effective action that have become commonplace in women's services during the last 20 years. The Minister of Justice is the only cabinet member who has responded to it by commenting on the reports proposals. While the annual consultations with the Ministry of Justice are important progress, they can have very limited effect without the cooperation of the other ministries involved, particularly Finance, Status of Women, Health and Immigration. In the NAC document, we call for funding to the national associations of transition houses and rape crisis centres. Virtually every national women's group endorsed that demand, but still the Status of Women department diverts money that should go toward fighting violence elsewhere. NAC has received no money for anti-violence work, nor has the Canadian Association of Sexual Assault Centres. Finally, no money has been made available for a national transition house conference.

Women have also asked for, and government has refused, the money to attend to the intersecting of oppressions: the extra burdens that racism and poverty add to gender-based violence and the extra and specific burdens of those living as lesbians or living with disability. In "99 Steps," and elsewhere, NAC has demanded an understanding that while all women are subject to sexist violence, some are more vulnerable both to male attackers who prey on them especially and to the racist and bigoted responses of the government and its institutions.

Men attack women with disabilities and women of colour more often than other women. In addition, the police and courts, social workers and hospitals do a less adequate job of dealing with this violence. Women's groups need money not only for making buildings accessible and for translation of materials but also for the costs of organizing as Aboriginal women, women of colour and poor women.

In its formal annual response to "99 Steps," the Ministry of Justice has limited discussion to the 56 steps that they might deal with as matters of law and order. The Liberals offered us changes to the Young Offenders Act to toughen treatment of teenagers. We responded that usually our attackers were full-grown men. We got the change to the Young Offenders Act anyway.

The Liberals offered longer sentences for crimes of hatred against women. We said all violence against women is hate crime against women. Furthermore, the treatment of men in prison send them out to us even worse than they went in.

The Liberals offered changes to processes so we could have speedy trials. We said that's fine but make sure the system does adequate investigations on these cases and bring these men into court for formal convictions. We got Bill C-41, which is allowing many men charged with violence against women to evade convictions and to evade reasonable sentencing. This cynical disregard for the need for real change and its substitution with a media campaign is heartless and deceitful governance.

LAW and ORDER ≠ EQUALITY

We warned against cuts to legal aid, but we got them. Women have no right to a lawyer to defend the custody of their children and to protect them from an abusive husband or father, or to defend their right to joint property, or even to defend themselves from criminal charges resulting from their self-defence. When they commit poverty crimes, prostitution and welfare fraud, they are underfunded for legal aid and risk severe punishments.

For three years women fought for some protection in law from unfair trial practices. Courts demand to see a woman's diary, counselling records, employment or education records. Women complaining of sexist violence should not have to prove themselves worthy of the protection of law.

Still, when feminist groups demand money for programs, the Liberals claim repeatedly that they cannot relieve the plight of abused women through social development. The Liberals have used the debt and deficit as excuses not to fund programs that would help fight violence against women and children.

This deficit hysteria has prevented the first and most fundamental step towards ending male violence: the government should encourage a transition house, rape crisis center and women's centre in every community. It must fund these centres not simply to treat victims but because the centres will help end the violence. In spite of the Red Book promise and the recent availability of money that could be budgeted for this purpose, the Liberals have refused to commit themselves to this objective.

In addition, the federal government should directly fund the equality seeking work of women's institutions. NAC and the Canadian Labour Congress endorsed the demand for $50 million to do just that. Across the country, women who joined the anti-poverty march agreed. In spite of the Red Book promises to make women safer and in spite of the recent additional sums of money available to spend, the Liberal government has also refused to meet this demand.

Instead, it has downloaded all such responsibility to the provinces. But federal officials have not obliged the provinces to comply with the Canadian Charter of Rights and Freedoms, which protects the rights of women. The federal government pretends it has no responsibility in this area while other lower levels of government deliver the fatal blows to social programs and to women's organizations. In Alberta, Ontario and BC, women-led services are under a dire threat. In the poorer provinces, women's services have never had government finances. On Aboriginal lands the federal government has prevented the establishment of women's services. The lack of these services is reflected in the lack of women's rights and in the plague of violence against women.

In the international arena, Canada brags of its treatment of women and offers itself as a teacher to other nations. However, NAC and many of its member groups like the OAITH do not believe that Canada is living up to those public agreements. Women are demanding an accounting at the UN.

The Convention for the Elimination of All Forms of Discrimination Against Women (CEDAW) states: "Take all appropriate measures to eliminate discrimination against women by any person, or organization or enterprise"; and "take all appropriate measures, including legislation to modify or abolish existing laws, regulations, customs, and practices which constitute discrimination against women." At the

Fourth World Conference on Women in Beijing, the following demand was made: "Provide adequate safety nets and strengthen state-based support systems" (Beijing Platform for Action).

Finally, in the alternative report submitted by non-governmental organizations (NGOs) represented by NAC to CEDAW, it was stated that "CEDAW and the Canadian Charter of Rights and Freedoms promise that equality. They legally bind the federal government to act in an equality promoting fashion and not to take measures which will defeat women's advancement."

The federal political parties have made it clear in this election that they would like to avoid dealing with the kinds of social development models that would end violence against women. They would like us to think that only law and order is effective; to believe that the only spending on women is to supply band-aid after-the-fact services funded by the provinces, if they are funded at all.

It is important that the government gets the message through the questions asked by us at All Candidates' meetings that violence against women is on the national agenda, whether they like it or not. Women's safety is protected by the Canadian Charter of Rights and Freedoms and affects the equality rights of more than half the national population. It is a matter of national importance. It is a matter that will help us achieve the kind of society we intend to have.

Questions:

1. Does your party support NAC's demand of $50 million to support feminist strategies to eradicate male violence against women?

Liberal Party (Liberals)
　　　Minister of Finance Paul Martin agreed to sit with NAC and find the $50 million in the budget. However, in December 1996 he backtracked significantly only to say that he would "work with NAC

and other ministers to see if he could find the
money."

Bloc Québécois
Failed to respond.

Reform Party
Failed to respond.

New Democratic Party
Failed to respond.

Progressive Conservative Party
Failed to respond.

2. Will your party ensure that there are adequately funded,
independent, women-controlled rape crisis centres, transition houses and women's centres in every community in the
country?

Liberal Party
Failed to respond.

Bloc Québécois
Failed to respond.

Reform Party (Reform)
Reform would favour devolving responsibility for
the establishment of rape crisis centres, transition
houses and women's centres to either provincial or
civic levels of government.

New Democratic Party
Failed to respond.

Progressive Conservative Party
Failed to respond.

3. Does your party support an amendment to the Divorce Act to include a preamble that would reflect a feminist-based analysis of power and of women's equality; an amendment that would acknowledge the pervasiveness of male violence against women in the family and note that men's violence maintains men's control over all aspects of family relations, including the acquisition of property and income and control over all of the most fundamental decisions relating to children and child rearing? The preamble would serve as a frame of reference for judges in the determination of family law issues, particularly on the issues of custody and access.

Liberal Party (Liberals)

Allan Rock, the Minister of Justice, said in the June 1996 "Consultation on Violence Against Women" report that he "doesn't rule out the prospect of a preamble to the Divorce Act as suggested." But he also said there are "no plans at this time to make any major legislative changes to the custody and access provisions of the Divorce Act."

Bloc Québécois

Failed to respond.

Reform Party (Reform)

Reform do not support this demand. In fact they claim that "strengthened enforcement of access orders ensures that even after divorce, children can benefit from as much as possible the participation of both parents as they grow up," and they claim that "the individual circumstances of each dissolving family are taken into consideration in rulings on support and access."

New Democratic Party

Failed to respond.

Progressive Conservative Party
Failed to respond.

4. Will your party repeal sections 9(2) and (3) of the Divorce Act that require lawyers to tell their divorcing clients about mediation services? (Mediation has come to mean the loss of legal protection for women and its substitution with bad social work. The 60 women's groups consulted by the government in June, including NAC, argued that mediation sells women out and denies our right to advocacy. We said mediation should not be in any legislation or family law policy. Mediation Centres should not be funded or promoted by the Justice Departments, the courts and the law. They should divert federal funds supporting mediation experimentation and research to fund legal aid, advocacy and support programs for women.)

Liberal Party (Liberals)
No. In the 1995 Department of Justice Response to 99 Federal Steps, the Liberals stated that they have "... no plans at this time to make any major legislative changes to the custody and access provisions of the Divorce Act."

Bloc Québécois
Failed to respond.

Reform Party (Reform)
No. The Reform Party will not repeal these offensive sections. Instead, Reform state that they "support the process of mandatory mediation."

New Democratic Party
Failed to respond.

Progressive Conservative Party
Failed to respond.

5. Where does your party stand on the request for a continued stay and for the granting of landed status to women who refuse to marry sponsors who have acted abusively? Currently, these women who have entered the country under the family-class are deported if the sponsor reneges on the sponsorship deal before marriage.

Liberal Party
>   Failed to respond.

Bloc Québécois (Bloc)
>   The Bloc do not support the government's practice
>   of deporting women who are fleeing an abusive
>   sponsor prior to marriage. The Bloc believe the dis-
>   cretionary power of the minister should be used in
>   cases such as these to allow women to remain in
>   Canada.

Reform Party (Reform)
>   The Reform Party would deport women who refuse
>   to marry their sponsor despite the violence.

New Democratic Party (NDP)
>   The NDP do not support the government's practice
>   of deporting women who are fleeing an abusive
>   sponsor prior to marriage. The NDP believe that
>   the perpetrator of the violence and not the victim
>   should be subject to penalties. The NDP would
>   work with women's groups to draw up suitable
>   changes to the Immigration Act and to immigration
>   policies.

Progressive Conservative Party
>   Failed to respond.

8

Health Policy

Anna Demetrakopoulos, Joan Grant-Cummings, Vuyiswa Keyi, Sabina Nagpal with Laurell Ritchie and Nandita Sharma

---

Jenny Williams is a member of the Inuk women's group and a volunteer at the women's shelter in Nain, Labrador. She is very concerned about the effects the huge Voisey's Bay nickel development is having on women and their families. The influx of mining officials is already causing a housing shortage in Nain. While there is an infusion of cash into the community, there is also an infusion of drugs. Sexual assault and abuse are on the rise. Jenny is worried about the spread of STDs and HIV/AIDS. Also, no Inuit women have been hired. While mining companies are making billions of dollars off their land, little of this is benefiting the community. Hunting patterns are being disrupted. Jenny and the women's group are calling for a long-term community development plan to protect the local Inuit and Innu peoples from this disaster in the making. Health, employment and social issues must be part of any environmental study.

Health: A Human Right

Most Canadians hold to the principle that healthcare is a right — not a commodity to be bought and sold on the market. At the time this guide is being written, it is less than two years since the Canadian government signed the Beijing Platform for Action at the Fourth World Conference on Women in Beijing, China. It was during the preparatory exercises for this conference that the government signalled to women a major shift in its thinking on health. Prior to this, the government was clear about the Canada Health Act principle of universal access to healthcare for all. In the preparatory exercises, Canada fought for the statement "Women have the right to the enjoyment of the *highest attainable standard* of physical and mental health" (para. 89, Beijing Platform for Action). There is an important distinction between health as a human right and "affordable" health. This statement, it was argued, would protect the government from litigation if women and their families demanded good healthcare for all. This statement suggests a price tag must be attached to "health."

Women have soundly rejected this approach and continue to validate healthcare as a human right. A 1996 study commissioned by the federal government and submitted to the National Forum on Health found that the vast majority of people in Canada continue to reject two-tier medicine or more family responsibility for care of the sick. Another study done by the research firm Ekos found that when people were asked to name "the aspects of health care of greatest importance to you" the majority chose "equal access for all Canadians" over all other options. In a similar question, Ekos asked whether people should be allowed to get faster treatment by paying extra. Again, the majority responded with a resounding "No!"

More women than men favour public healthcare. These are many reasons for women's support. First, women know that they will bear the brunt of the loss of public Medicare. It will mainly be women who will pick up the slack in the wake of the destruction of public healthcare. We know that it is women who are generally held responsible for taking care of ailing family and community members. Already, women in the paid labour force take more days off than men in order to fulfill domestic responsibilities. With cuts to health services, this will only worsen. Second, it is mainly women support staff and women nurses who are losing their jobs as these services are cut.

Third, we know that the services required specifically by women have historically been the least well-funded. For instance, breast cancer, one of the primary killers of women, is on the rise. Canada has the second highest rate of breast cancer in the world, exceeded only by the US. The number of new cases has more than doubled, from 6,900 in 1969 to 18,600. It is estimated that 5,300 women die every year from breast cancer. Very little money is available for research and most of it goes to finding a cure. But researchers still do not know what causes breast cancer or how to prevent it. This situation will not improve if our public healthcare system is gutted.

Clearly, the majority, and especially women, support a public healthcare system where society as a whole takes responsibility for the ailing. People in Canada want to make sure that medical care is equally available to all — whether rich or poor, whether well-connected or not.

This principle is enshrined in the five main conditions of the Canada Health Act: universality, portability, accessibility, public administration and comprehensiveness.

If the provinces fail to meet these five conditions, the federal government has the power to withhold money for healthcare. This power ensures that there are reasonably comparable levels of services and access to services across the country. In the end, it is the only way for the federal government to enforce national standards for Medicare.

In a January 10, 1997 letter to NAC, Health Minister Dingwall wrote: "As Prime Minister Chrétien has recently stated, without national standards and enforcement by the federal government, Medicare will die. Canadians expect and demand that Ottawa will defend the health care system, and that trust will not be betrayed." But nothing could be further from the truth!

Dr. Judith Kazimirski, president of the Canadian Medical Association, states that "the single most important reason for the deterioration of the system is the significant and ongoing decline in federal financial support for health care funding" (*Toronto Star*, 18 November 1996, "Health care goes under microscope").

With the cut of billions of dollars in transfer payments to the provinces under the new Canada Health and Social Transfer (CHST), the Liberals have seriously jeopardized the government's ability to uphold national standards. Simply put, it takes federal money to maintain the principles of the Canada Health Act: "no cash, no clout!"

Already, over $7 billion in cuts have been made in social program spending. To make matters worse, over the next two years the Liberals will slash more than $3 billion from federal cash transfers to provinces for health, welfare and post-secondary education. By the year 2000, the Liberals will have cut $11.1 billion from federal transfers, effectively cutting federal support in half from the levels in April 1995.

As a result of Liberal government actions, people in Canada currently face a national crisis in healthcare. No community is immune. Downsizing of hospitals and hospital closures, reductions in direct health services and loss of extended healthcare services are the obvious symptoms. The everyday assaults on human rights and dignity in the lives of women and their families are impossible to measure.

With the cuts in federal government spending on healthcare has come a loss of public confidence in the public system. Little by little, people in Canada are becoming more frustrated with a public system that is dying the death of a thousand cuts. This is exactly what the right wing and their friends who would profit from privatized healthcare want. With the loss of public confidence comes pressure for a two-tier healthcare system.

As of March 1997, nine of the ten provinces — the exception being Quebec, whose government wants sole power over healthcare — are planning to rewrite the rules governing Canada's healthcare program with the help of the federal government. In closed door negotiations between the federal and provincial governments, there is talk of allowing greater provincial "flexibility" in the delivery of Medicare, thus risking greater disparities between regions of the country. Ultimately, all of the premiers want to end Ottawa's ability to enforce national Medicare standards. They tell us that people in Canada would still have national standards, only now these standards would be jointly enforced by the provincial and federal governments. But, this is not what joint enforcement will mean. Instead, it will allow provincial governments to privatize Medicare while passing the buck and beginning healthcare's long descent to the bottom.

Instead of joining forces and demanding that the federal government provide adequate funding for a national public healthcare system, many of the provincial governments are using people's frustration with an inadequately funded system to grab federal powers. Some provinces are trying to eliminate the federal government's role in setting national standards by ending its ability to enforce them through the Canada Health Act. Alberta Premier Ralph Klein has gone so far as to say that provincial compliance with national standards should only be "voluntary." Klein argues that a private or two-tier healthcare system would improve people's lives.

The idea that a privatized, two-tier system of healthcare will improve people's lives is wrong. A Harvard University study recently found that people in Canada pay $272 per person for healthcare administration and overhead for a public healthcare system. People in the US, however, pay $615 per person in US dollars for a two-tier system that leaves about 40 million people without any medical coverage at all! In fact, the American privatized, two-tier healthcare system is the most expensive system in the world! Another study done by the Agri-Food Competitiveness Council found that "American employers pay anywhere from three to five times more than Canadian employers to fund employee health and social benefits — and that includes the taxes they pay for those benefits in Canada." Finally, an American government study concluded that by adopting Canada's single-payer system, the US could save enough money to provide free coverage for the estimated 40 million Americans currently without health insurance.

Weakened National Standards and Privatization

To make matters worse, two further developments, also encouraged by federal government cuts in spending on healthcare, now present a fundamental threat to the well-being of Canada's Medicare system. First, there is the drive to commercialize services and shift from a non-profit model to a for-profit one. Second, there is a move to substitute community-based services with multi-national enterprises.

As a result of pressure from the medical establishment and some of the biggest corporations selling private insurance, brand name drugs, health data management and biotechnology, our governments are starting to shrink the core of services guaranteed by the Canada Health Act and to re-interpret "medically necessary" services.

Aided by the federal government's massive funding cuts, some provincial governments have already begun to privatize labs, as well as hospital and nursing services, and have slashed their list of covered services (called de-listing). Some reproductive health services, perhaps the most significant and frequent reason women turn to the healthcare system, have been among those de-listed.

Services that are not covered would be open to privatization and commercialization. The same kind of two-tier system that exists in the US — one for the "haves" and one for the "have nots," many of whom will be women — would be created. Excluded services would be available only to those who could afford to pay directly or buy private insurance, which was the case in Canada before the 1960s. The provisions of the North American Free Trade Agreement (NAFTA) allow American corporations to move in on these privatized services, operating for example as "medical inns" or "managed health care providers."

Already, private healthcare is becoming more and more common across Canada. The portion of healthcare purchased from private businesses is now over the 28 percent mark. Private businesses are lining up to cash in as the federal government gives up its responsibility to truly enforce the Canada Health Act's principle of "comprehensiveness" and to provide public Medicare. Currently, the purchase of healthcare services from private businesses is the fastest growing segment of healthcare financing.

Objections to "for profit" healthcare models are based on more than principle. They will greatly increase public spending on services covered by Medicare (consider the out-of-control prices for drugs used in hospitals) as well as the overall public and private spending that goes to healthcare. Someone has to pay for those profits. And for those who are shut out, it could be a matter of life or death.

The following is a brief overview of the situation of public healthcare across Canada:

British Columbia

- The procedures covered under Medicare have been reduced.

- Hospitals have been "downsized," beds reduced and nurses laid off around the province.

- In 1995, the government changed the provincial drug plan and created a list of pharmaceutical categories for which the government would cover only the cheapest medications. In 1997, drugs treating high blood pressure will be added to this list.

- Physiotherapy services cost a $7.50 user fee for the first 12 visits. After that the cost rises to $8.25 per visit.

- Every week, six patients are forced to go to the US for cancer treatment because the waiting lists in BC are too long. This costs the government $1.5 million a year.

Alberta

- Alberta's healthcare spending has been slashed by $515 million. Only after a massive public outcry did the Tory government cancel its plans to cut another $123.5 million from the healthcare system in 1996.

- Premiums for healthcare have almost doubled in the past five years, causing great difficulty for many individuals and families.

- Five hospitals have been closed across the province.

- The number of nurses employed dropped from 19,033 in 1992 to 10,758 in 1995. This drop is a 43 percent decrease. An Alberta committee of doctors stated that basic care had been made impossible by the cuts.

- Alberta allowed the establishment of semi-private medical clinics and it was only after the federal government withheld federal funds and fined Alberta $3.4 million for allowing private clinics that Premier Klein backed down.

- Klein opposes the federal government's duty to place financial penalties on those provinces that fail to uphold national standards.

- Alberta is planning a pilot project on a concept known as "capitation," which would force patients to pledge loyalty to a single doctor. The Alberta government's plan would financially punish patients who seek the advice of other doctors by making them pay for the service of the new physician from their own pocket.

This action would contravene the standards of the Canada Health Act.

Saskatchewan

• Saskatchewan's annual healthcare budget has been reduced by more than $33 million from 1991.

• Fifty-two small rural hospitals have been closed since 1993.

• Prior to 1993, Saskatchewan had the highest ratio of acute-care hospital beds in Canada (4.6 per 1,000 population). Since then, the number has shrunk to 3.34 acute-care hospital beds per 1,000 population.

Manitoba

• Hospital beds have been cut and more closures are planned.

• The availability of certain services, such as obstetrics, will be reduced by centralizing them in certain locations.

Ontario

• The federal government has slashed its funding of healthcare in Ontario from 52 cents of every Medicare dollar in 1980 to 32 cents in 1996.

• User fees for drugs (seniors people on welfare); $2 per prescription (subsidized rate) or $100 for everyone else.

• In the last five years, 25 percent of all acute-care hospital beds have been closed. There are further plans to cut another 25 percent of all acute-care beds.

- Ontario's Tory government cut hospital budgets by 18 percent over three years. Hospitals are already dealing with $1.3 billion in provincial funding cuts.

- Ontario's Tories hand picked a "restructuring committee" and empowered it to shut down or merge hospitals throughout the province.

- An estimated 15,000 nurses in Ontario could lose their jobs due to hospital cutbacks, closures and mergers.

- Ontario is planning a pilot project on a concept known as "capitation," which would force patients to pledge loyalty to a single doctor with financial penalties for those who seek the advice of other doctors.

- Contracting out of community long term nursing care services such as homemaking and personal care to allow more private, for-profit companies to compete for contracts. Contracts will be awarded based on quality with reasonable price.

Quebec

- Quebec's Tory government's three-year freeze on the healthcare budget was the equivalent of a $1.4 billion cut in healthcare.

- Quebec's health minister reduced the length of hospital stays, resulting in a 300 percent increase in day surgery.

- Seven hospitals are to be closed throughout the province. Twelve more hospitals are being merged or transformed into long-term geriatric-care centres.

- 4,000 of 23,000 hospital beds are to be shut down.

- 13,300 jobs in healthcare are to be eliminated.

New Brunswick

- In some hospitals, bed spaces have been slashed by 50 percent.

- Hundreds of healthcare and support staff have been laid off.

Nova Scotia

- The provincial government has embarked on a slash and burn approach to its healthcare budget. After public outcry, the government increased its 1996/97 health budget by $65 million.

- Hospital beds have been slashed by about 33 percent.

- Five hospitals have been closed and turned into community health clinics.

- Day surgeries have increased.

- Women have had to reduce the amount of time spent in hospital after delivering their babies.

- A recent government survey indicated that 62 percent of people in Nova Scotia believed that the quality of healthcare in the province is worse than it was five years ago.

Prince Edward Island

- Federal government reduced its transfer payment for health, education and welfare by $15.1 million.

- Money for acute-care has been cut.

- So-called "community-care" remains underfunded.

- 200 healthcare workers were forced into accepting severance and early retirement packages.

Newfoundland

- Hospital beds have been slashed by almost 30 percent since 1990.

- In St. John's, the Liberal provincial government plans to close three of eight hospitals.

- The government plans to lay off 300 hospital workers.

Northwest Territories

- Federal funding has been cut 5 percent.

- Follow-up visits by patients to doctors in the territorial capital or in southern Canada are no longer routinely covered, forcing follow-up to be done over the phone.

- When the NWT is divided into an eastern Inuit-dominated territory of Nunavut and a western territory, Ottawa states that no additional money will be allocated, thus significantly reducing the quality and availability of healthcare.

Yukon

- Yukon's health budgets have grown from approximately $1,740 to $1,790 per person.

Given that this is what is happening across the country, no wonder that, in its final report, the National Forum on Health found that people in Canada "... fear a society in which a growing number of people are marginalized from the economic and social life of their communities." The Forum adds a final warning to the Liberal government that "should universal access be compromised, the game is over — Medicare as we know it will be gone." It concluded by saying that "[the situation] does not have to come to that. Equitable access and high quality are achievable, provided certain changes are made." (*Toronto Star*, February 1, 1997, "Free drugs urged in health overhaul.")

The very personal issue of health is a public priority for all women and for our families. Before the recent round of cuts in the 1990s, the healthcare system was inadequately serving the majority (women, people of colour, Aboriginal peoples, people with disabilities). Statistics show that people who are struggling against systemic barriers have poorer health.

With the real threat of privatization of services, it will soon be harder to get good professional care. Women who are already doing double-duty as wage earners and mothers will be forced to provide greater care for their families. Part-time and contract workers without benefits and unemployed people will face greater stress when they are without proper care and unable to pay their bills. Few women have workplace prescription drug plans for themselves and their children; others are excluded from company plans because they are part-timers.

Using the UN Platform to Build a National Women's Health Strategy

In 1987, the Canadian government signed a UN agreement that said that it was time to look at health differently. This agreement suggested that the whole picture of a person's life (her income, education, family and gender) was important in determining the quality of her health. Thus it is known as the World Health Organization (WHO) social determinants approach to health. This approach represented a big switch from the biomedical approach to health, which focuses on a person's illness and treats it separately from everything else in her life. Under the biomedical model of health, which still exists, most people are treated when they are already sick. In the WHO model of health, "Prevention and Health Promotion" are more than just buzzwords; they are actively pursued.

United Nations health policies established that social spending in all areas that affect people's standard of living would also improve people's health. Many countries that spend more than Canada on social services, such as education and employment, spend less on direct health.

Unfortunately, this UN agreement is one more great idea sitting on a shelf. Governments have gone in the opposite direction and have cut away many of the services that maintain a basic standard of living and contribute to overall wellbeing. The federal government in Canada took drastic action by cutting the transfer of funds to the provinces, creating the current healthcare crisis. The Canada Health and Social Transfer underfunds existing health services and does not ensure our health rights, while provinces decide how to most cheaply repair the old system.

The documents signed by Canada as part of UN processes, including the Beijing Platform for Action, are important for women, especially as they confirm what many of us already suspected.

We have to create a strategy that helps women to link their personal health issues. We can build a common picture of the healthcare systems that will be appropriate for women's different needs.

Women's health activists have called for a national women's health strategy that would:

- make progress in the critical areas;

- identify the people hardest hit by ongoing service reductions;

- support local, regional and provincial networking amongst issue-specific groups;

- promote women's participation in health reform and work for democratization of the healthcare system;

- plan for long-term changes to bring the social determinants of health and cultural appropriateness into the mainstream delivery of services.

On the positive side, years of lobbying by women's health activists have resulted in some research and networking dollars. Health Canada has funded five new research centres on Women's Health and the Canadian Women's Health Network, which will operate a national clearinghouse from the Women's Health Clinic in Winnipeg. The needs of Aboriginal women, women of colour, lesbians, immigrant and refugee women, young women and women with disabilities are not well addressed in the program of the Centres. As usual, women from these communities will have to work to ensure access to and control over the research and to influence the research priorities. Women working together is the only way to make change and hold governments accountable.

Some political issues seem to distant too our lives, but high quality, appropriate healthcare services need to be close to our homes.

The Environment and Women's Health

The Red Book states that the Liberal government will use the review of the Canadian Environmental Protection Act to make pollution prevention a national goal and to strengthen the enforcement of federal pollution standards.

NAC recognizes that the greatest impact of environmental pollution is on those who are least able to afford the health, economic and social costs of such a burden: poor women, working-class women, Aboriginal women, lesbians, women with disabilities and women of colour.

In 1995, the Canadian Environmental Protection Agency (CEPA) was reviewed. Only one of the ten members of the Standing Committee on Environment and Sustainable Development, a committee that considered public presentations on the review of the CEPA, is a woman. Since a large proportion of the burden of environmental degradation falls on women, it is imperative that women, especially women of colour, Aboriginal women, lesbians, women with disabilities, poor women and working women play a key role in environmental decision-making.

In our presentation to the Standing Committee, NAC requested that the Canadian Environmental Protection Act should incorporate the "precautionary principle" as defined in the Rio Declaration as follows:

Where there are threats of serious or irreversible damage, lack of full scientific certainty shall not be used as a reason for postponing cost-effective measures to prevent environmental degradation.

We strongly believe that all environmental decisions, including both pollution prevention and remediation, should be guided by the precautionary principle. It is ultimately more cost efficient — and results in the least impact on health and the environment — to focus on pollution prevention as opposed to focusing exclusively on the remediation or cure of ailments.

It is now well-known that wind and water carry pollutants generated by industry or waste disposal thousands of kilometres away from their points of origin. Many researchers and activists have noted the correlation between rising rates of breast cancer and the proliferation of the nuclear and chemical industries following the close of the Second World War. About 16,000 new cases of breast cancer are diagnosed in Canadian women every year, and about 6,000 of these women die of the disease. Breast cancer is the leading cause of death for women between the ages of 35 and 55.

Inorganic food grown in Canada and imported from outside Canada is also a source of environmental pollutants, adding to the daily burden of toxins our bodies must bear. The food is sprayed with a number of pesticides. Outside Canada, pesticides that are restricted from use in Canada are often used. According to the US Attorney General, 95 percent of pesticides used on residential lawns are considered probable or possible carcinogens by the US Environmental

Protection Agency (EPA). Pesticides and herbicides, also known as "xeno-extrogens," act as endocrine disrupters, causing a wide range of health problems such as neurological and behavioural disorders, birth defects, reproductive failures and damage to the immune system, in addition to cancer.

After approximately 50 years of chemical use, it is now evident that the cost of approving a substance for use without appropriate testing and then attempting to control or mitigate the adverse impact on human health and the environment is significantly greater than the cost of upfront screening. NAC recommends that mandatory pollution prevention be required by enforceable regulation with appropriate penalties upon non-compliance. In addition, there should be a clear and transparent process for public input into any environmental legislation that is proposed or amended.

Hazardous waste represents another environmental challenge to women's health. Canada is the world's largest per capita producer of toxic wastes. On average, at least 4,000 tons of toxic wastes are exported to Asia every day. Ninety percent of this waste and that exported to all countries of the South and of Eastern Europe comes from the member countries of the Organization for Economic Cooperation and Development (OECD). Media attention and lobbying from environmental and progressive groups led to the Basel Convention on the Control of Transboundary Movements of Hazardous Wastes, signed after a long political struggle in March 1994. The Basel Convention calls for an immediate ban on all exports of hazardous wastes destined for final disposal in non-OECD countries, and a phase out, by December 31, 1997, of exports of hazardous wastes intended for recovery/recycling in non-OECD countries.

Questions:

1. Will your party oppose any increase in "for profit" health-care services?

Liberal Party (Liberals)

The Liberals state that they have no intention of permitting privatized medicine.

But the Liberals have cut more than $7 billion in funding to the provinces for health, education and social programs. And the Liberals plan to slash another $ 4.3 billion dollars in federal transfer payments to the provinces for social spending. The level of federal government support for the healthcare system will have been effectively cut in half by the Liberals from April 1, 1995, to April 1, 1999.

At the same time, Health Minister David Dingwall has stated that the public healthcare system can stand no more funding cuts! In other words, the Liberal government would like to be seen as the great defender of Medicare while stripping it of much needed funding.

Bloc Québécois (Bloc)

The Bloc are in favour of maintaining the five principles of Medicare inside Quebec. The Bloc state that "… it is essential and urgent that Quebec take over the administration of the [healthcare] system in its entirety, including financing."

Reform Party (Reform)

The Reform Party's plan for healthcare is to transfer money to the provinces without placing any restrictions on how the provinces spend the money on healthcare. This would allow provinces to permit private, "for profit" healthcare. The Reform Party is actively discussing user fees, facility fees and private clinics.

In 1995, Reform MP and critic for healthcare Dr. Grant Hill stated his approval of a private healthcare system. He stated that "If you want a Mercedes in health care, you would get private insurance, pay for it out of pocket or get a loan. You

do not expect taxpayers to pay for a Mercedes."
(*Vancouver Sun*, February 3, 1995, "Health-care
cuts vital, Reform agrees.")

New Democratic Party (NDP)
The NDP oppose increasing "for profit" healthcare
services.

They state that they will "... refuse to allow
Medicare to be privatized and butchered by the
right-wing political agenda of past Conservative
and present Liberal governments ... [and] will fight
the move towards two tier health care at every opportunity ... [They] will continue to pressure both
the federal and provincial governments to work towards a more intelligent approach to health care
which acknowledges the importance of preventive
and community health, strong social programs, and
jobs in ensuring the health of Canadians."

Progressive Conservative Party (Tories)
Tory leader Jean Charest is in favour of de-listing
some health services by taking them out of the public system.

2. Does your party support a call for increased federal health
transfers to provinces?

Liberal Party (Liberals)
No. Health Minister David Dingwall says that there
is "... no commitment to bump up the transfer payments."

Bloc Québécois (Bloc)
The Bloc state that "... it is essential and urgent
that Quebec take over the administration of the
[health care] system in its entirety, including financing."

Reform Party (Reform)

Sometimes yes, sometimes no. In the lead up to the
1993 federal election, Reform promised that they
would not cut spending on healthcare. By 1995, Dr.
Grant Hill, Reform MP and critic for healthcare,
stated in the *Vancouver Sun* (February 3, 1995) that
"there must be spending cuts and program reductions in all areas." By 1996, Reform were once
again promising to increase spending on healthcare
and education by $4 billion (no break down on how
much for healthcare given) even as they were promising to cut current spending by $15 billion.

New Democratic Party (NDP)

Yes. The NDP "fully support maintaining federal
cash transfers at a level adequate to protecting and
strengthening Medicare" and would indeed use the
powers under the Canada Health Act, including the
withholding of funds, to ensure that provinces uphold the five basic principles.

Progressive Conservative Party (Tories)

No. In their latest policy document, the Tories identify the elimination of the federal deficit as their priority. They plan to achieve this through spending cuts.

3. Would your party support a call for national standards to
be maintained and enforced under the Canada Health Act,
with a strong role for the federal government in the interpretation and enforcement of those standards?

Liberal Party (Liberals)

Prime Minister Chrétien has stated that he will not
give up the federal government's duty to enforce
Medicare standards enshrined in the Canada Health
Act.

But, as critics charge, through the massive cuts in
federal support for healthcare, the Liberals have

placed in jeopardy Canada's universal healthcare system.

Bloc Québécois (Bloc)
The Bloc are in favour of maintaining the five principles of Medicare inside Quebec. The Bloc state that "... it is essential and urgent that Quebec take over the administration of the [health care] system in its entirety, including financing."

Reform Party (Reform)
Reform favour a two-tier medical system where the public system dwindles and is diminished into a substandard service for the poor and a private one is established for those who can afford it.
Reform would only ensure that minimum care standards are enforced. Reform did not specify which services would continue to be provided by a public healthcare system and which would be delisted and privatized.

New Democratic Party (NDP)
The NDP support the maintenance of national standards and will enforce the five principles of the Canada Health Act through the federal government's withholding of funds to provinces that fail to comply with the Act. They add that the NDP are "committed to maintaining and ensuring that this system continues to serve all Canadians."

Progressive Conservative Party (Tories)
The Tories state that "national standards for social programs should no longer be dictated by the federal government."
They believe that "basic standards" should be up for negotiation between the provinces and the territories and the federal government with the federal

government playing no role in enforcing national standards.

4. Women living with AIDS/HIV continue to be overlooked. They need primary care, hospices, prevention and research. Will Health Canada provide adequate funds for HIV-positive women's involvement in addressing these problems?

Liberal Party (Liberals)
The Liberals have stated that the current $40-million-a-year funding for AIDS research and support for victims will expire in the spring of 1998 and will not be renewed.

Bloc Québécois
Failed to respond.

Reform Party (Reform)
The Reform Party state in their official policy that the party "... believes that AIDS is a very serious disease. Reform commits to providing adequate funds for both this disease and all other diseases that affect Canadian women. We believe that there would be criteria set out which would prevent one disease becoming politically popular."

They add that "these criteria would include: the severity of the disease — that being morbidity and mortality, the likelihood of a cure, the expertise of research in Canada, the number of resources that are available from other sources such as private sources and the age groups affected. These criteria would see AIDS well funded, with ongoing funding that would be satisfactory to everyone."

New Democratic Party (NDP)
The NDP state they will continue to call for a national strategy aimed at research, treatment and prevention of AIDS that would include a strategy for

women living with AIDS and that would provide
funding for primary care, hospices, prevention and
research. The NDP state that they will insist upon
the involvement of women and men living with
HIV/AIDS in the development of this strategy.

Progressive Conservative Party
Failed to respond.

5. Will your party ensure the inclusion and implementation
of the precautionary principle, by ensuring that no substance
is approved for use unless it is clearly determined that there
is minimal impact on human health and the environment?

Liberal Party (Liberals)
The Liberal Party conducted a public review of the
CEPA in 1995. The Liberals tabled a new CEPA in
the House of Commons on December 10, 1996, to
replace the old Act. Critics have stated that the new
act appears to weaken the CEPA and is not what
the House of Commons Environment Committee
called for last year. Groups from many indsutries
have lobbied to ensure that many of the suggestions
to strengthen the regulations are not incorporated
into the amended Act.

Bloc Québécois (Bloc)
The Bloc support the precautionary principle, but
believe that the provinces are the ones that should
implement it.
The Bloc support the principle of the complete
removal of toxic waste from the environment, but
again promote the need for an absolute agreement
between the provinces and the federal government
in order to achieve the main purpose: better health
and a clean environment.

Reform Party (Reform)
> Reform are generally not in favour of environmental protection as they state they have not yet developed an analysis of the long-term economic effects of environmental toxins.
>
> But Jim Abbott (Kootenay-East) indicated to a reporter of *The Globe and Mail* that "Canadian business people are already weighed down by too much 'green tape'", in response to the Liberal initiative to set up a green watchdog for the environment.

New Democratic Party (NDP)
> The NDP state that they have "always supported the precautionary principle" and a strengthened CEPA.

Progressive Conservative Party
> Failed to respond.

6. What steps has your party taken to implement the ban and phase-out of hazardous waste trade as per the Basel Convention?

Liberal Party (Liberals)
> The Liberals have indicated that Environment Canada, in consultation with interested parties, will review this issue and develop recommendations on how to implement the decision of the parties to the Basel Convention.

Bloc Québécois (Bloc)
> The Bloc state they are committed to support all laws forbidding trade of toxic waste between Canada and other countries, particularly developing countries. The Bloc state their support for the Basel Convention and that they will consistently pressure the federal government to honour all their commitments.

Reform Party
> Failed to respond.

New Democratic Party (NDP)
    The NDP support the Basel Convention's ban on importing and exporting hazardous waste.

Progressive Conservative Party
    Failed to respond.

The following questions were raised by NAC's Health Committee and Environment Committee. However, the responses that we received to these questions were insufficient for our purposes. They do remain important for women to consider when questioning those parties seeking their votes.

7. What will your party do to improve access to information and support for women who live with breast cancer?

8. Health services for immigrants, refugees and migrant workers are currently restricted under a 1993 Interim Federal Health Plan. Will your party replace this legislation in consultation with immigrant and refugee women's organizations?

9. Holistic healing systems include naturopathy, acupuncture and shiatsu, traditional Aboriginal health models, yoga and many other practices from different cultures. More women are turning to holistic healing systems after they have exhausted medical attempts to address their health problems. Will your party support the funding of alternative holistic healthcare services under Medicare?

10. Will your party explore a fully funded National Drug Plan to ensure equal access to medications and supplements such as vitamins?

11. Reproductive and genetic technologies will be legislated and regulated by the government. Decisions about regulation need to include those most affected by the technology (women, people with disabilities, Aboriginal people). How will your party ensure the participation of those most affected in the development of legislation, regulation and research, including public review of Canada's involvement in the Human Gnome Project?

9

Women and Postsecondary Education

Maureen Trotter

Alice is 37 years old, the single mother of two children. She lives in a small city in central British Columbia. She supported herself and her children for many years with a small dog-grooming business. Four months ago she was in a car accident and now suffers chronic back problems. She has had to close her business and her savings were depleted. She is now on social assistance. She needs to be retrained for a less physically demanding career. She has always wanted to be a teacher but she would need to move to a larger city which has a university and she would need about $75,000 in student loans to complete the five-year degree. This option is risky and she would be in debt for many years afterwards. She is not sure what she should do. She and her children face many years of poverty whatever choice she makes.

Women have been coping with a decade of funding cuts in public postsecondary education. Even so, in 1993 and 1994, total federal government funding, cash and tax credit transfers, accounted for more than one-half of funding for postsecondary education in Canada. This funding is increasingly disappearing as the federal government cuts transfer payments to the provinces under the Canadian Health and Social Transfer (CHST). As a result, student tuition fees are rising and will continue to rise in order to cover the shortfall. As tuition fees increase, fewer students can afford postsecondary training. In 1996, for the first time in Canada, enrollment in postsecondary educational institutions declined.

In an attempt to offset the anticipated increase in tuition fees, the federal government announced changes in the federal student program. Student loans are to be more readily available and they are to be paid back on an Income Contingency Repayment plan. This means that if the student's income is low, lower monthly payments would be required. This would hit women and children the hardest. Higher income earners, mostly men, can pay their loans off more quickly, thus paying less interest. Women in lower income jobs (or taking time out to raise children) would pay longer and, ultimately, substantially more with the accumulated interest. Some estimates suggest that it could take up to 35 years to repay the debts, making it impossible to save to buy a house or for future retirement.

Compounding the problem are the cuts to social program spending. As the provinces are pushing to get people off the welfare rolls, they are no longer supporting welfare recipients who wish to return to school. In many parts of the country, women with small children who want to upgrade their educations or training are forced to take out large student loans, which come with no guarantee of employment after graduation. The training that social assistance recipients are required to take by some provinces is focused on short-term job search skills and not on providing real education and training for life-long careers. Consequently, poor women are increasingly trapped in the cycle of poverty.

For the first time in the history of Canada, Aboriginal people are entering the postsecondary system in significant numbers; at precisely the same time, funding for these students has been capped. Similarly, students of colour are increasing in numbers and are also facing reduced per capita funding, adding to the barriers they face in Canada. Reduced funding for educational institutions has a significant impact on the quality of education. With uncertain yearly funding, institutions have a reduced ability to plan ahead. Part-time and temporary instructors are being used to replace permanent ones. These instructors often have less experience, little preparation time or paid marking time. We are also seeing reduced funding for library services and a decline in both student support services and the maintenance of buildings. Many institutions are no longer covering the costs of such services as learning assistance and assistance to students with disabilities. Class sizes are increasing with less help available to students from instructors.

As institutions are required to rely more heavily on student tuition fees, there is an increased need to compete for students, especially as the number of people who can afford to attend postsecondary education declines. More money is being spent on student recruitment and advertising and less on books or instructors.

Institutions, both the postsecondary and the kindergarten to Grade 12 systems, are increasingly looking to private corporate sponsors for funding. This may result in some programs being well funded and others that are of little interest to corporations being poorly funded. Programs with high enrollments of women (for example, nursing, education and social services) are less likely to benefit from corporate funding and will become poorer and poorer. Programs that do receive corporate funding will be subject to the increased control of corporations. We already see that research of benefit to corporations makes up the proposals that most often receive funding.

Less revenue from government will make cohesive public policy on education more difficult. Public educational standards will become more difficult to enforce and public accountability will be increasingly eroded. Provinces will increasingly go their own way and there will be even less likelihood that national standards for education will be a concern. Already, Quebec has discussed the existence of differential fees for in-province and out-of-province students.

Private, for-profit training and educational institutions are cropping up across the country. Control is being taken by small groups of people to use in their own interest. Disparities among institutions are increasing. This shift to the privatization of education follows the same shift occurring in social services and healthcare. Education is increasingly being considered a commodity to be bought and sold on the open market (where students — the consumers — are charged as much as possible and the instructors are paid as little as possible and required to work longer hours with fewer resources). Promoting equality is not an objective of privatized education.

The idea of education as a human right, as a social necessity, essential to a fair and prosperous country, is being eroded. Postsecondary education and training is becoming accessible only to students who can afford it or those who can afford to incur large debts; the rest are left behind. Ultimately, this results in an increase of inequality — between the rich and poor, between Aboriginal and immigrant students and the rest of the population, between provinces and between men and women.

Affordable, accessible, high quality, universal public education at all levels is a major component of the democratic society we are working towards building in Canada. Dismantling public education through underfunding or privatization is a step towards dismantling democracy.

We need:

- Education funding to be restored to at least 1994/95 levels.

- The federal government to begin immediately a national review of the funding and delivery of postsecondary education and training.

- Creation of a separate federal funding program for postsecondary education where provinces are held accountable for spending.

- Federal standards for the delivery of high quality, accessible, universal public education and training.

Question:

Would you support the restoration of funding for postsecondary education to the provinces to at least 1994 levels?

Liberal Party (Liberals)
> Although the student enrollment in postsecondary institutions increased throughout the 1980s, the Liberals reduced the growth in transfer payments to 6 percent (less than half the rate of inflation). In 1994, the Liberals extended the 1990 freeze instituted by the Conservatives indefinitely. Now with the CHST, the transfer payments are being drastically cut. Provinces are reeling under the impact.

Bloc Québécois (Bloc)
> The Bloc want control of education within Quebec.

Reform Party (Reform)
> The Reform party has supported the idea of private "Charter schools" and is on record supporting the devolution of responsibility for programs to the provinces and supports cutting transfer payments.

New Democratic Party (NDP)
> The NDP is opposed to the massive cuts made to federal transfer payments for social programs, healthcare and education.

Progressive Conservative Party (Tories)

In 1986, the Conservative government reduced the growth in transfer payments by 2 percent, costing the postsecondary education system $1.6 billion over the next five years. In 1990, the Conservatives froze transfer payments at the 1989/90 levels for two years.

10

Childcare Policy

Martha Friendly

A woman in Nova Scotia tells about her experience: ... *For me, as a single mother, not being in the labour force is not an option. In the last five years, I've worked at all kinds of jobs ... cashier, factory, cleaning ... whatever I could get, and whatever wasn't being downsized. At the same time, I've been really aware of how much my kids need to be in a good, stable situation while I've been away from them ...someplace where they'll not only be safe and fed but will be happy and learn. I don't have any relatives here in Canada who can help me out, so childcare outside my family is my only option. My older son ... now four ... has been in all kinds of childcare, and some of it has been pretty awful for him ... Once I discovered that the sitter who was looking after him had nine others! And twice I had really good care for him where he was happy but both times, they had to stop looking after him.*

Now I not only have another child ... a two-year old ... but I'm finishing a great training program with a promise of a good job at the end. For the first time, I have a chance to get into work that pays well, and has good hours. The problem is ... childcare again. Since I've been in the training program, both my kids have been in a really good childcare center where my government subsidy has paid most of the cost. But when I finish the training program, the subsidy will *end. I'll be expected to pay full-fee ... about $1300 a month for both kids. There's no way I'll be able to pay that even on a better salary than I'm used to. A single parent can't cover the full cost of care ... not unless she's a doctor or lawyer! So it'll be back to the childcare circus again. Doesn't the government care what happens to kids?*

Although childcare has been a key issue for the women's movement since the 1970s, Canada has never developed a coherent way of providing reliable, high quality childcare. Childcare has always been too inadequately funded and supported to become widely available or affordable.

The Childcare Situation in 1996

Canada is almost alone among industrialized nations in having no coherent plan for high quality childcare/early education that supports women's equality, children's healthy development and well-being and family security. The delivery and management of Canadian childcare has always been under provincial/territorial jurisdiction, and there are numerous variations in funding arrangements, regulations and the range of services offered. No region of Canada has a satisfactory program that ensures adequate affordable, high quality childcare.

The prospects for good childcare looked rather promising in the mid-1980s. All jurisdictions had childcare regulation, all offered funding, at least for selected families, and almost all had universal funding schemes for regulated services (albeit some were very small). Nationally, annual increases in the supply of regulated centre-based childcare rose as high as 23.43 percent in 1984, 14.63 percent in 1986 and 16.96 percent in 1988. These developments suggested that governments had begun to acknowledge their role in ensuring health and safety at a minimum, that they recognized that the quality of childcare was important and that they had an emerging appreciation of childcare as an essential service for families across the social and economic spectrum.

In the 1990s, however, this potential was reversed. By the mid-1990s, the childcare situation was in decline in much of

Canada. Universal funding had been eliminated or decreased in a majority of jurisdictions and fee subsidies for low income parents had been reduced, frozen and capped by provincial/territorial governments. Standards and supervision of care had been reduced in a number of provinces. Expansion of regulated childcare slowed to its lowest annual increase rates since 1983.

In most of Canada, there has been a retreat from a conception of childcare as an essential public service. Even in the few provinces that have maintained the status quo or have made some improvements, the government initiatives have not been assertive or comprehensive enough to even begin to keep pace with the demands of the times. Although the birthrate has dropped in some parts of Canada in recent years, the number of children who are assumed to need childcare because their mothers are in the labour force has continued to grow.

Corporate and government downsizing and cutbacks mean that more women work non-standard hours and at part-time, seasonal or non-standard jobs. The piecemeal, unreliable, user fee–based nature of Canada's childcare funding situation mitigates against the provision of childcare to match these employment circumstances.

Thus, the Canadian childcare situation, never a strong one, has been diminished, downsized, privatized and deregulated in much of Canada.

Childcare and the Liberal Record

Following the 1993 federal election, advocates were cautiously optimistic. In the Red Book, the Liberals promised to spend $720 million on 150,000 additional regulated childcare spaces to be cost-shared with the provinces over three years, following 3 percent growth in GDP.

Ultimately, however, the Liberals' agenda of cost-cutting and the devolution of power to the provinces has meant not only that the commitment to expansion has not been kept but that childcare has been left immeasurably weaker than it was before 1993.

The 1994 federal budget earmarked funds to meet the Red Book's first two years of childcare spending: $120 million and $240 million to be spent in 1994/95/96. Most of these funds were not spent. The Social Security Review in 1994 again highlighted the need for a national childcare program. Instead, the 1995 budget abolished the Canada Assistance Plan (CAP), the sole federal/provincial cost-sharing program. CAP's existing childcare funds — the only federal funds for regulated childcare — would be subsumed under the new Canada Health and Social Transfer. The CHST, a block funding arrangement to transfer federal funds to the provinces, would encompass health, postsecondary education and welfare and would be subjected to massive federal cuts. These shifts would effectively remove the federal government from the social policy field.

Thus, not only did the federal government not spend the funds committed in the Red Book and the 1994 budget, but existing funds used for regulated childcare were eliminated as well. With the elimination of the CAP, the federal financial base for regulated childcare, existing or new, disappeared.

Federal/provincial discussions about childcare continued even after the federal government announced that it would devolve responsibility for social programs to the provinces. Even while these were ongoing, the federal government generated an "exit strategy" for its Red Book commitment to childcare in early 1996, arguing that provincial governments hadn't demonstrated sufficient interest. The 1996 Throne Speech formalized the barrier designed by the federal government that would mitigate against progress in childcare: in the future, new national programs would not be initiated without the agreement of a majority of provinces.

In the provinces, the federal withdrawal from the field has contributed to a policy environment in which "anything goes." The Harris government's radical attacks on childcare in Ontario, as well as the more subtle erosion in, for example, Newfoundland, Prince Edward Island or Manitoba, are part and parcel of the federal retreat as well as of provincial downsizing. Finally, the prohibition against new national programs means that it is unlikely that a national childcare plan will emerge in the near future.

Thus, not only has the Chrétien government not met its election commitment to expand childcare but also Canada's childcare situation has become remarkably frailer than it was before 1993. As community-based childcare services diminish and childcare becomes ever more fragmented and more targetted, the vision of a national childcare program — of high quality and accessibility to all — becomes more distant.

NAC and Childcare

For NAC, the establishment of a childcare system is of the highest priority. NAC's childcare policy is based on three principles:

- Access to childcare should be universal and equitable. All children, regardless of family income, region of the country, ability or disability, ethnic, linguistic or racial background or work status, are entitled to accessible, culturally sensitive and appropriate high quality childcare.

- A childcare system should provide comprehensive services. Different families, children and communities have varying childcare needs. In order to meet these needs, a range of options, planned at the community level, should be available.

- Childcare must be high quality. Childcare that is regulated, non-profit and pays its staff adequately is more likely to meet this criterion.

NAC advocates childcare as a public service system that receives government funds directly. We do not support the use of public dollars to pay individual parents through the tax system or vouchers to purchase childcare, as this tends to favour wealthier parents and does nothing to provide childcare spaces for those who need them.

Maternity and Parental Leave and Family Leave

A comprehensive system of childcare should be complemented by adequate maternity and parental leave and benefits. Leave for new parents (maternity and parental leave) and family leave to care for sick children, spouses or other dependents are critical issues concerning women's equality at work.

Maternity and parental benefits are paid for 15 and 10 weeks respectively through Unemployment Insurance and have been cut every time UI benefits are cut. As well, fewer and fewer women are eligible to receive UI benefits. Today women on maternity leave receive only 55 percent of their salary. This is one of the poorest programs in the countries of the North.

NAC believes that maternity and parental leave should be paid at 95 percent of earnings and that the benefit period should be lengthened. As well, NAC advocates 10 days of paid family leave per year. This would provide a more secure income for pregnant women and encourage more men to take advantage of parental leave to care for their children.

Question:

Is your party prepared to launch a national childcare program within a year of your election with national objectives and guidelines to ensure the quality, availability and affordability of childcare services consistent with the principles adopted by NAC and its partners in the childcare movement?

Liberal Party (Liberals)
    No. The Liberals state that "federal discussion on childcare will be consistent with the directions set forth in the Speech From the Throne — in that the federal government will not use its spending power

to create new shared-cost programs in areas of exclusive provincial jurisdiction without the consent of a majority of provinces and that provinces choosing to opt out of such a program would be eligible for compensation provided that they have equivalent programs."

Bloc Québécois (Bloc)

The Bloc state that they do not "deny to Canada the right to establish a national child care network, if a consensus to that effect emerges among the provinces. This should, however, in no way affect Quebec's autonomy in this field."

Reform Party (Reform)

Reform's policies on childcare seem to be targetted at encouraging women to stay at home.

Reform is committed to extending the Child Care Deduction to all parents: $3,000 for every child 7 to 12 years of age, and $5,000 for every pre-school child.

The Reform strategy is to also give a tax reduction that would mainly benefit the so-called "traditional family," where the male works outside the home and the woman is economically dependent on the man.

New Democratic Party (NDP)

Yes. The NDP are committed to the creation of a national childcare program, restoring funds cut by the Liberals, and adding 150,000 regulated spaces over four years, with the federal government carrying 40 percent of the cost of the program.

Progressive Conservative Party (Tories)

The Tories will introduce a childcare tax credit.

11

Women and Work

Lorraine Michael, Leah Vosko and
Laurell Ritchie

There is a deepening economic crisis in Northwestern Ontario, with increasing poverty for women (70 percent of people living in poverty are women). In this region women are being affected by the restructuring of the economy, which is driving them into unemployment, insecure employment, underemployment or part-time employment with inequality caused by sexism, racism and class becoming more severe as the jobs become more scarce. Increasingly, women in Northwestern Ontario are being strapped into poverty with cuts across the board, including legal aid, welfare, and so on. With inordinately few decent paying jobs, which provide economic independence in our area, women and their children have little opportunity to get out of poverty.

Susan, mother of two, lost her job when the company where she worked moved out. She is looking for a job in an area that has 12.4 percent unemployment and where women receive barely half of the wages that men earn. The few jobs that do show up on the local listing are for part-time, minimum-wage jobs. She has completed three job-training programs, but there are no jobs in these fields.

Labour Market Policies

Labour market policies designed to encourage "flexibility" for employers are on the rise. These policies are put into place to reduce the regulations that business operates under. Such policies have been advocated by such international institutions as the Organization for Economic Cooperation and Development (OECD) and the International Monetary Fund (IMF). These new policies support a "just in time" workforce where workers' schedules are erratic and where workers are laid off at will. A "just-in-time" production model has also driven the contracting-out of jobs in virtually all sectors from hospital administration to auto parts. "Flexible" work practices also include non-standard pay policies, such as those used in the garment industry, where homeworkers are paid on a piecework basis and excluded from standard benefits and social protections. Most of these workers are immigrant women.

In the paid labour market, women are working harder and their real wages are falling. To make matters worse, men have received most of the scarce high-wage jobs created in Canada. In 1995, women working full time averaged 70 cents for every dollar earned by men working full time. A growing trend in many workplaces is to hire new employees at a wage rate that is lower than the regular rate for current employees, resulting in a two-tier workforce in both union and non-union workplaces. This is especially harmful to young women just entering the paid labour force.

Furthermore, standard definitions of economic contributions completely ignore unpaid domestic labour. Women continue to perform the bulk of household work in Canada, contributing two-thirds of the total unpaid work that is done in this country. Married women perform three-quarters of the unpaid work of all women in Canada. Statistics Canada calculates that unpaid work was equivalent to anywhere from 32 percent to 54.2 percent of Canada's GDP in 1992.

No Jobs! No Jobs! No Jobs!

High unemployment is one of the consequences of the Liberal government's broken promise of "Jobs! Jobs! Jobs!" We are witnessing "jobless growth." Layoff notices fly fast even as corporations report record profits. Take for example the case of Canada's biggest banks. With after-tax profits of more than $6 billion in 1996, they still laid off thousands of women.

The unemployment rate has hit the double digit mark several times since 1993. Over 1.5 million people are officially unemployed. Hundreds of thousands more are forced to rely on meager welfare checks. Many, many more live with the daily fear of losing their jobs.

On average, Aboriginal women face an official (and underestimated) unemployment rate of 17.7 percent. But unemployment rates for Aboriginal women living on-Reserve are regularly 30 percent to 80 percent. For women with disabilities the unemployment rate is 19.1 percent and for women of colour it is 13.4 percent. Young women suffer from the highest unemployment rates of all. If we include those who have simply been discouraged from looking for work, the unemployment rate for young women would be above 20 percent.

Underemployment

Since 1977 the number of women holding more than one paid job increased by 372 percent. In 1993, women whose main job was less than 30 hours a week accounted for more than 70 percent of all workers holding down more than one job. Only 20 percent of paid women workers have full-time, full-year jobs that pay more than $30,000 per year. While 70 percent of part-time jobs are held by women, one-third of these women would prefer to have full-time paid work.

Self-Employment

Three out of every four new jobs created in the 1990s have been in the form of self-employment. Most of these are in small businesses. In the past 10 years the number of self-employed women has risen. Ten years ago the rate of women running small businesses was 32 percent and now it is 38 percent. The rate of women running their own corporations rose to 23 percent from 18 percent. At the same time, both 1995 and 1996 broke previous records in the number of bankruptcies filed in Canada. Self-employed workers work longer hours with very little time off. Most self-employed women work 10 hours or longer per day. These women work six or seven days a week. These hours do not include the unpaid work in the home. Most domestic work is done by women.

Cheap Labour Strategy

The Liberal government's absurd response to high unemployment was to restructure and cut $5 billion from the Unemployment Insurance account. As a result, the number of unemployed workers receiving UI plummeted from 89 percent in 1990 to only 50 percent in 1996.

As part of the overhaul of UI (which the government now calls EI), an hours system was established. This system will negatively impact the entitlements of workers working 15 to 34 hours per week, most of whom are women.

If provincial/federal negotiations result in new provincial powers over pregnancy and parental benefits, these two hard-won universal entitlements under the UI Act could be transformed into "needs-tested" welfare benefits.

Another one of the Liberal government's responses to high unemployment is workfare. With the introduction of the Canada Health and Social Transfer (CHST), forced work for welfare is no longer seen as a denial of a person's right to food and shelter. In some programs, such as New Brunswick Works, women have been the focus of programs verging on workfare. The promise at the end of the rainbow is jobs and training. The promise is not kept. The real outcome is the introduction of another cheap labour strategy.

Employment Equity

In December 1995, Bill C-64 was put into place. It is the updated version of the Employment Equity Act (EEA). According to the Act, Employment Equity is supposed to "achieve equality in the workplace and to correct conditions of disadvantage experienced by certain groups." These groups include women, Aboriginal peoples, persons with disabilities and members of visible minorities. For the first time, the EEA covers public sector as well as private sector employees in the federal jurisdiction. Women who work in banks, the federal government, communications, mail services, airlines and broadcasting are federal jurisdiction workers.

Downsizing in the federal public sector is counteracting the small gains made in employment equity. Also, it is the employee's responsibility to prove that discrimination exists. At least one federal department (Public Works and Government Services Canada) reports that groups affected by employment equity "are being declared surplus at a greater rate than other employees." Most employees covered under the EEA are in clerical and blue-collar jobs. These are the jobs most affected by downsizing. Under EEA, employees will have few rights in the face of job loss.

Questions:

1. Will your party affirm the right to refuse work for welfare?

Liberal Party (Liberals)
The Liberals consider the CHST the way to work with the provinces and Canadians to develop the values, principles and objectives that should underline a social union. The CHST removed protections against workfare that existed under the former Canada Assistance Plan.

Bloc Québécois (Bloc)
The Bloc support the right to social assistance based on need.

Reform Party
Failed to respond.

New Democratic Party (NDP)
> The NDP support the right to social assistance based on need.

Progressive Conservative Party (Tories)
> The Tories feel that social programs should be linked to "education, skills training and the labour market." They believe that "incentives are required to ease the transition of recipients from assistance to self-sufficiency."

2. Will your party support higher standards in the Canada Labour Code currently under review? In particular, will you support a) greater protections for part-time, temporary and teleworkers; b) tighter provisions on hours of work and overtime; c) extending the right to file a complaint of "unjust dismissal" to all workers, and d) the reinstatement of a federal minimum wage to be set at $7.85?

Liberal Party (Liberals)
> In putting forward Bill C-35, An Act to Amend the Canada Labour Code, the Liberals state that "any changes to the provincial and territorial general adult minimum wage rates are to be incorporated as the new federal minimum wage rates, as these are established from time to time." The regulations to do this came into effect on July 17, 1996.

Bloc Québécois (Bloc)
> The Bloc state that they are satisfied with what the Liberal government has done in this area.

Reform Party
> Failed to respond.

New Democratic Party (NDP)
> The NDP state they will fight for equal pay and benefits for part-time workers, the right to refuse overtime

work, incentives to redistribute working time and a review of all federal legislative provisions that encourage employers to schedule overtime rather than hire
new employees.

Progressive Conservative Party
Failed to respond.

3. Will your party support job creation through federal infrastructure spending? If so, would you bind the provinces to a)
employment equity requirements in spending their share of the
dollars; b) a 50/50 split between traditional physical infrastructures and new social infrastructures such as childcare?

Liberal Party (Liberals)
The Liberals are considering another infrastructure
program but have failed to build in employment equity requirements or to commit adequate resources to
social infrastructure as well as physical infrastructure.

Bloc Québécois
Failed to respond.

Reform Party (Reform)
Reform failed to respond to the issue of a federal
infrastructures program. However, Reform would
destroy employment equity legislation by repealing
section 15(2) of the Canadian Charter of Rights and
Freedoms. Section 15(2) allows governments to pursue special measures for "the amelioration of conditions of disadvantaged individuals or groups ...
because of race, national or ethnic origin, colour, religion, sex, age or mental or physical disability."
    They state that they will "discontinue federal af-
firmative action and employment equity programs."

New Democratic Party (NDP)
> The NDP state that they have long supported job creation through infrastructure programs, and that they would broaden the concept of infrastructure to incorporate investment in social and environmental measures such as
>
> • retro-fitting of public buildings, of older housing and of existing utility services for energy and water conservation;
>
> • construction of non-profit and cooperative housing to address the shortage of affordable rental housing in every major city in Canada;
>
> • development of community-based, not-for-profit childcare and elder care services.

Progressive Conservative Party (Tories)
> No. The Tories believe that only the private sector, not governments, should create jobs.

4. Will your party revoke the new UI "hours system" if part-timers working 15 to 34 hours weekly suffer a loss in UI entitlements?

Liberal Party (Liberals)
> The Liberals' record shows that they favour the new discriminatory system.

Bloc Québécois
> Failed to respond.

Reform Party
> Failed to respond.

New Democratic Party (NDP)
> The NDP state they will fight for

- • a new UI program that provides real support for every unemployed Canadian, with a target of replacing two-thirds of average earnings;

- • better integration of provincial training programs and UI, so that UI recipients will be encouraged to retrain while on UI and benefits will be extended where appropriate to permit people to complete training and educational programs begun while on UI.

Progressive Conservative Party (Tories)
The Tories feel that eligibility for unemployment insurance should be based upon "total amount earned for the year." They further believe that unemployment insurance should "... no longer attempt to serve the broader objective of income transfer."

5. Does your party believe that the good health of society should not depend on the unpaid labour of women as caregivers and that it is the responsibility of government to offer universal and comprehensive health and social programs? If so, will your party put more money into health and social spending with the demand that provinces reinstate funding where programs and services have been cut?

Liberal Party (Liberals)
The Liberals' policies have increased the amount of unpaid work women are held responsible for doing through drastic cuts in federal spending on social programs and services that help to alleviate the unpaid work women do. They have also failed to provide a national, public childcare program.

Bloc Québécois
Failed to respond.

Reform Party (Reform)

No. The Reform Party would cut all federal payments for welfare programs, ultimately end the Canada Pension Plan, eliminate federal responsibility for maintaining national standards for healthcare and other social programs, reduce employers' contribution to unemployment insurance benefits and through its tax policies "encourage" women to be economically dependent on men by staying at home.

Reform continue to insist that "... individuals, families and communities" should "lead the way to growth, progress and unity."

New Democratic Party (NDP)

The NDP state they "believe the health of a society should not depend on the unpaid labour of women as caregivers. They believe also that governments have a responsibility to ensure that the basic needs of citizens are met. Programs that help people in need require stable, ongoing funding. They must be regulated and measured to ensure they are effective, accessible and accountable. The role of caregivers must be specifically addressed in this process."

Progressive Conservative Party (Tories)

The Tories state that "social programs should be designed on the premise that responsibility for the well-being of citizens rests first and foremost with the individual and family."

6. Will your party protect the integrity of the parental and pregnancy benefits as universal entitlements under the UI Act and ensure that no level of government transforms it into a "needs tested" welfare benefit?

There were insufficient responses from the federal parties to determine their position but this is still an important question to ask those seeking your vote.

12

Pension Policy

Laurell Ritchie with Monica Townson,
Ruth Rose and Jo-Ann Hannah

Rich Seniors?

In 1996, the average senior family income was about
$40,000 but fully 79 percent of seniors received less than
that amount. One out of every five seniors lives in poverty. Among the single elderly, most of them women, the
poverty rate is still 50 percent. Not all seniors go golfing;
many struggle to pay for food and rent and to get transportation to their doctors. Class is an issue. And so too is
the status of women in our society.

Nowhere is the attack on our universal and non-profit social
programs more evident than in the federal restructuring of
our public pension system. Between the two extremes of the
very poorest and the richest members of society lies a great
chasm of moderate income earners who are increasingly left
to fend for themselves. For women, that spells poverty.

Not so very long ago, poverty among elderly women was
at crisis levels, a great failure of our modern welfare state.
In 1980, a shocking 70 percent of older women were surviv-
ing on income that was below official poverty levels. As
advocated by NAC and other organizations, the Old Age

Security (OAS), the Guaranteed Income Supplement (GIS) and Canada Pension Plan/Quebec Pension Plan (CPP/QPP) programs were improved so that by 1993 the poverty rate among senior women, though still far too high, had dropped dramatically to 45 percent. Seniors' poverty still has a gendered component: twice as many women as men are poor, especially after age 75. Among the gains was an opt-out period that allowed parents to exclude up to seven years of full-time childcare when calculating their average earnings for CPP/QPP.

Now the financial health of our public pension system is the subject of public hysteria, driven by government and corporate propaganda. The public is not being given the facts.

The CPP/QPP system is *not* going broke. It can't go broke because it is a pay-as-you-go system with premium adjustments every five years to cover benefit payoffs. Each new generation pays for the pensions that go to their parents, knowing their society has established laws that ensure the next generation pays for their pensions.

Some believe that the CPP/QPP must be cut because of government deficits. They don't realize that the CPP/QPP does not involve any government spending. Workplace premiums fully fund the plan.

The Conservative and Liberal Strategies

Following the lead of the Conservatives in the late 1980s, the Liberal government is continuing to dismantle our public pension system by stealth. It began in 1989 with an OAS clawback from higher income seniors, a move calculated to appeal to the average pensioner but actually the first step towards eliminating universal entitlement. Without universality, public support erodes and it becomes easier to reduce benefits. The obvious alternative to the clawback would be a more progressive tax system that applies to all income, whether from pensions, work or investments.

The federal government also positioned Registered Retirement Savings Plans (RRSPs) at the centre of a privatization strategy, increasing the amount that could be contributed yearly by individuals on a tax-free basis.

Now the federal government proposes to go to a "Seniors Benefit" that would replace OAS, GIS, the Age Tax Credit and Pension Income Tax Credit, and "means test" the entire package. The Seniors Benefit would take full effect in 2001, with only those 60 and older at year-end 1995 having an option to choose between the new system and the current one.

As a means-tested benefit, the Seniors Benefit would end the universality of Old Age Security. It would be "welfare for seniors." For married seniors, benefits would be based on the combined income of the two spouses. Middle income earners would lose most.

Spouses with no employment history would no longer have a retirement benefit in their own right. Women whose spouses have income over a $40,000 threshold will have their benefit check reduced or eliminated, a throwback to an era when women were dependent on their husbands' income and there was an assumption that family members share family income equally.

There has been no special impact studies of the effects on women and workers of colour, nor upon workplace pension plans that assume current public pension entitlements.

Public Pension Spending

Canada's spending on public pensions as a portion of Gross Domestic Product is one of the lowest in G-7 nations and less than half the average of advanced industrial countries in the OECD (Organization for Economic Cooperation and Development). Canada's "payroll taxes" for CPP/QPP in 1993 were only 4.6 percent; far below the US rate of 12.4 percent or Germany's rate of 17.5 percent.

Who Wins?

The planned restructuring of the public pension system is to the advantage of Bay Street's private investment industry and the banks. They are the declared enemies of the public system for the simple reason that they can't make a cent from public pensions. The investment industry and banks clearly stand to gain from the transfer of billions of dollars from public, non-profit plans to the private RRSP accounts from which they make millions.

The RRSP system primarily benefits the higher income earner. By 2005, someone earning $86,000 (3 times the average earnings of women workers) will be able to contribute $15,500 to an RRSP. That means a tax refund of about $7,750 — almost double the annual OAS benefit now paid to seniors.

The government itself admits that these tax subsidies for a relatively small part of the population cost the public purse about $15 billion a year in lost tax dollars, not counting the cost to provincial governments. Compare that with the $15 billion spent in 1991 to provide OAS/GIS to the benefit of virtually all seniors.

In 1995, only one-third of eligible tax filers contributed to an RRSP. A Royal Trust spokesperson explained: "Primarily, Canadians are still finding it economically difficult — in their personal circumstances — and they basically just don't have the money to make their contributions." (*Toronto Star*, December 4, 1996, "RRSP plans take beating, survey shows.") Moreover, the majority of people making withdrawals on their RRSPs are not seniors but people under 45. They are doing so just to make ends meet — not to retire.

Who Loses?

Privatizing our public pension system by cutting public pensions will *not* save money; it will merely shift the burden to the individual.

The middle income Canadians who contribute to RRSPs are increasingly drawing down those accounts during periods of unemployment and financial hardship, minimizing their small tax advantage and jeopardizing their retirement income.

Pension privatization has particularly negative effects for women because women have low earnings, live longer and work in sectors and jobs with increasingly precarious em-

ployment and little in the way of pension plans. This means
that most women cannot afford private pension savings.

Taking It Further: The Reform Party

Preston Manning's Reform Party takes the Liberals' and
Conservatives' game plan a step further. Reform openly
advocate "private sector solutions," the same ones that have
served women so poorly. Their proposed "Super RRSP"
would replace the public CPP/QPP. It is modelled on a
program introduced by the Pinochet dictatorship in Chile.
Organizations such as the Canadian Life and Health Insurance Association have promoted similar ideas.

If tax-deductible RRSPs replaced the CPP/QPP, we
would see in effect a massive transfer of wealth from lower
income tax payers, mostly women, to higher income tax
payers, mostly men. Half of the tax advantages for RRSP
contributions and private pensions go to the top 10 percent
of tax payers, few of whom are women.

Real Problems and Real Solutions

The real problems in funding our public pension system lie
with massive unemployment and underemployment as
well as the protracted periods of high real rates of interest
on our national debt. Social program spending accounted for
only 6 percent of the increase in the national debt since 1975;
50 percent was in tax breaks to the wealthy and 44 percent
in high interest rates.

An ageing population may mean an increase in contribution
rates, but other factors such as full employment, improved
wages and economic growth can minimize those increases by
lowering the ratio of retirees to active workforce participants.
As well, there are well-considered proposals for improving our
public pensions in the 1996 Alternative Federal Budget formu-
lated by popular sector organizations and economists.

Women's Pension Rights

The universal OAS program is essential for women; we
should oppose a family-income tested model. We must en-

sure that the burdens of "cost control" do not fall mainly on women and that we retain women's right to an independent retirement income.

The CPP/QPP system is clearly a candidate for improvements: benefits should be increased to 50 percent of average earnings with an annual maximum and stronger "drop out" provisions for women. The CPP/QPP has also been of immeasurable benefit to women and should be defended because it provides:

- benefits indexed to inflation, important given the longer life expectancy of women;

- a guaranteed benefit rate and less risk than with private RRSPs;

- low earning years and years devoted to full-time childcare, which can be excluded when calculating a benefit rate;

- a lower payment per dollar of retirement benefit for low income earners.

- access for women to a share of their husbands' benefits;

- portability from one job to the next and from full-time to part-time work;

- survivor and orphan benefits if a husband dies before retirement;

- very low administration costs compared with private plans;

- democratic control through Parliament and re-investment in Canada.

These benefits of the public system cannot be reproduced by a private pension model.

Furthermore, a woman would need to contribute 18 percent of income for about 40 years in order to get a decent retirement income from RRSPs, something most women can't afford. In 1992, only 21 percent of women contributed to RRSPs, largely due to their low pay.

The restructuring proposals that are being advanced will have very negative effects on women. Our system of public, non-profit pensions, first introduced in the 1960s, is one of Canada's greatest social achievements. It is the most important reason for the declining poverty rates among older women.

Questions:

1. Will your party strengthen the public pension system and maintain women's independent access to OAS?

Liberal Party (Liberals)
> The Liberals will lower the income level at which benefits are subject to "clawback."
>
> By 2001, they would combine OAS and GIS as a "Seniors Benefit" that would be income-tested based on family income, ending the universality of the OAS program and eliminating women's independent access to public pensions.

Bloc Québécois
> Failed to respond.

Reform Party (Reform)
> Reform would replace guaranteed OAS with an income-tested model.

New Democratic Party (NDP)
> The NDP would make no changes to the current OAS.

Progressive Conservative Party (Tories)
> The Tories would continue to support OAS as an income contingent plan.
> They would also eliminate the current non-taxable seniors benefit.

2. Will your party strengthen the CPP/QPP?

Liberal Party (Liberals)
> The Liberals have recently proposed changes in the CPP that would reduce some benefits. Although they did not go as far as they had proposed earlier, these reductions may be a step towards other benefit cutbacks in the future.
> Significantly, the Liberals are now proposing that CPP funds be handled by the private sector, a clear step in the direction of privatization.

Bloc Québécois
> Failed to respond.

Reform Party (Reform)
> Reform would abolish CPP/QPP and employer contributions and set up a mandatory "Super RRSP" program operated by private financial institutions. The "Super RRSP" is modelled on a 1981 scheme implemented by the Pinochet dictatorship in Chile, where workers are required to contribute 10 percent of their income to funds operated by private corporations that take 25 percent of the funds as operating fees.
> Reform would also eliminate the "drop out" provisions and end benefits for disability and death and for survivors and orphans.

New Democratic Party (NDP)
> The NDP would increase CPP contributions in line with other industrial countries and increase the benefit rate for low income Canadians.

The NDP would strengthen the "drop out" provision to take account of a precarious labour market.

They would re-invest public pension moneys in the Canadian economy, restrict foreign investments and restrict private insurance firms from dumping disability cases onto CPP/QPP.

Also, the NDP would pursue a full employment policy.

Progressive Conservative Party (Tories)

The Tories state that "the size of our national debt combined with the future costs of pension ... raises serious question about whether ... these commitments can be sustained." Specifically, the Tories are calling for:

• raising CPP/QPP contributions;

• reducing existing benefits;

• investing CPP/QPP contributions in private capital markets under private management;

• encouraging savings through RRSPs, employer-based Registered Pension Plans and Deferred Profit Pension Plans;

• moving orphans' benefits, disability benefits, etc. out of the CPP/QPP and having these programs funded separately.

13

Justice Policy

Colleen Hua and Amy Go

When my husband and I separated, the money was not there for me to get a lawyer. I do not receive child support and my husband has unlimited visitation with the children at his convenience. I got some information on my rights and know that I need to go to court. I do not qualify for Family Legal Aid because there is no abuse present and it is not a child welfare case. I really want to get this all settled, but I cannot afford the legal fees. I feel very frustrated that there is no representation for people like me. There needs to be increased funding to Family Legal Aid in Prince Edward Island so that all Island women, like me, can access the judicial system to settle their disputes.

By reducing funding for legal aid, Canadian governments are in effect denying justice to women. Women often do not have the resources to fight lengthy legal battles in courts, or take other avenues against their partners to seek custody, or to take court action against their employers to stop harassment in the workplace.

Denial of legal aid is only a part of broader erosion of social, economic and political rights faced by women. Drastic cutbacks to funding and the erosion of national standards on health, social assistance and services have seriously put women's physical, financial and social well-being in jeopardy. Women workers are also paying a higher price when employers cut jobs, wages and benefits in order to cut costs. When employers are given more power from different levels of government to lower employment standards and deregulate requirements to provide "favorable conditions" for business, women workers are made vulnerable to exploitation.

In the face of such serious violations of women's rights, the Canadian human rights framework is ineffective. It is outdated and has not kept pace with the changes in society. Particularly, the human rights framework does not address the erosion of social and economic rights. For example, the growing number of women working at home at less than minimum wage find it difficult to turn to the Human Rights Commissions to address the systemic violations that they are facing. Given that Canada's human rights framework is primarily a system driven by individual complaints, it has never adequately addressed systemic violations and discrimination.

The Canadian Human Rights System

In 1996, the Liberal government did amend the Canada Human Rights Act (CHRA) to include sexual orientation as a source of discrimination. However, amendments to the CHRA on sexual orientation do not ensure equality for lesbians under all federal legislation. For example, the CHRA does not cover equality rights of lesbians under the Income Tax Act and the Pension Benefits Standards Act. In order to guarantee full and equal rights for lesbians and gays in Canada, the government must also explicitly recognize same-sex couples as families.

Facing tremendous barriers in the political arena to effect policy changes, more and more equality seeking groups are turning to the courts and using the Canadian Charter of Rights and Freedoms as their tool to hold the government accountable for its actions. The Charter was entrenched in the Canadian Constitution in 1982. However, suing the government is costly.

The Court Challenges Program was developed by the Government of Canada. It ensured that equality protections contained in section 15 of the Charter were accessible whether you had money or not. The program provided money for test cases that dealt with these protections. Despite the success of the program, it was cancelled in 1992. However, in 1993, the Liberals restarted the program. The mandate of the Court Challenges Program covers only federal policies, legislation and practices. In light of the fact that many important areas such as health, education and social services are primarily within provincial jurisdiction and that the federal government is giving more power to the province and is abdicating its responsibility to uphold national standards, women need funding support from a Court Challenges Program that can help them challenge the right-leaning provincial governments.

Even though using the Charter is one way of upholding women's rights, many have doubts about the ability of our court system to do so. The Canadian judiciary has been dominated by a conservative ideology. At a group level, the male-dominated judiciary has not shown a good understanding of the systemic inequality faced by women, particularly those who face multiple forms of discrimination. At an individual level, recent events highlighted the lack of fairness to women as victims or defendants.

The system is based on judges not holding discriminatory attitudes. Little is done to ensure this, however. Only extreme cases of bias come to the attention of the public. Very little continuing education is provided for the judges. Judges are appointed and given independence on their rulings. Training in equity issues is not mandatory.

Little progress has been made to appoint women, Aboriginal peoples, people with disabilities or people of colour as judges. As of October 1, 1996, only 164 of the 988 federal judges were women — about 17 percent. The federal government does not even keep statistics on the number of visible minority judges.

Our justice system has particularly failed women who are incarcerated. Women in prison are victims of battery, incest, rape, poverty, homophobia, racism and abuse. People became more aware of prison conditions after the videotape of the April 1994 strip search of prisoners at the Kingston Prison for Women was played on national television. The inquiry, headed by Justice Louise Arbour, that followed this event made the public even more aware. The Arbour Inquiry and the videotape documenting the abuse suffered began to undo the belief that prisoners deserve punishment. It began to undo the idea that those in prison are being rehabilitated.

It costs tax payers about $92,000 a year to keep one women in federal prison. This does not take into account the costs of policing, legal aid, parole, probation and prison construction. The right tend to see prisons as "dumping grounds" for the poor, for people of colour, for Aboriginal peoples and for dissenters. They argue that these people are threats in order to convince us of their law and order agenda. In reality, the prison system is an industry in Canada. There has been a move to have prisons run by private companies. This has been done in the US by corporations like Wacken-hut. Companies who run prisons make profits by reducing the quality of food and by reducing staff wages by getting the unions out.

A good alternative to prison is community-based pro-grams. This approach costs less and is more effective. Un-fortunately, the law and order agenda prevails in governments' strategies in dealing with criminal justice. For example, changes to the Criminal Code were proposed by the federal government to deny the right to early parole for people serving life sentences. The federal government has also proposed legislation to establish a national DNA Data Bank. It is unacceptable that the government slash funding to feminist advocacy and support services that really do address male violence against women while putting money into expensive policing programs/systems like DNA testing.

Questions:

1. Will your party support the Court Challenges Program and increase transfers to provinces to ensure the viability of their

legal aid plans as well as effective access for disadvantaged groups?

Liberal Party (Liberals)
> The Liberals support the Court Challenge Program as is. They have never committed to the extension of the mandate to include other provinces.

Bloc Québécois
> Failed to respond.

Reform Party (Reform)
> Reform want to get rid of the Court Challenge Program.

New Democratic Party (NDP)
> The NDP support the Court Challenge Program and would agree to consider extending its mandate to include other provinces.

Progressive Conservative Party (Tories)
> The Tories state: "Generally, the right to be judged has always been a rule of law in Western societies, so yes. But when you start discussing transfer payments, things become very delicate. We have to do more and more with less and less so we would be reticent to say yes."

2. Is your party in favour of strengthening judicial accountability given the recent cases where perceived bias of judges was found? If so, what mechanisms would your party implement to ensure a high national standard of judicial impartiality?

Liberal Party (Liberals)
> Even though the Canadian Judicial Council is required by statute to investigate and inquire into all allegations and complaints about the judiciary, be-

tween 1990 and 1996 only two formal public inquiries have been held.

On the issue of education of judges, the Liberals only refer back to the Canadian Judicial Council, whose work it is, in part, to do educational work. However, the Liberals make no commitment to improving their work or the composition of this group.

Bloc Québécois
Failed to respond.

Reform Party
Failed to respond.

New Democratic Party
Failed to respond.

Progressive Conservative Party (Tories)
On the issue of education of judges, the Tories say that they "will make judicial education mandatory." However, they are not specific about the content of these educational reforms.

3. Will your party call a public inquiry to look into why Aboriginal peoples and people of colour are so heavily over-represented in the criminal justice system?

Liberal Party (Liberals)
The Liberals ended the "Aboriginal Justice Fund" on March 31, 1996. This fund provided money for the development of programs and services, public legal education, cross-cultural training, research studies related to Aboriginal justice issues and consultations undertaken by national Aboriginal organizations.

Bloc Québécois
Failed to respond.

Reform Party
> Failed to respond.

New Democratic Party
> Failed to respond.

Progressive Conservative Party (Tories)
> The Tories state that any public inquiry would be part of a bigger picture inquiry only. In partnership with provinces and territories they are interested in a coherent look at how the justice system is failing — that would be one of the components that could be looked at.

The political parties did not respond to many of the questions raised by the Justice Committee. We suggest that you raise them at All Candidates' Meetings.

1. Is your party in favour of including social rights (for example, adequate food and shelter) in the Charter?

2. Is your party committed to implementing the recommendations from Justice Arbour's Commission of Inquiry with respect to women in prison, specifically around issues of living conditions, discipline and security?

3. Will your party fight against any action to reinstate capital punishment?

4. Does your party favour alternatives to incarceration as a form of rehabilitation?

5. Does your party favour encouraging alternative justice mechanisms or systems for Aboriginal peoples and other culturally distinct groups?

6. Will your party support high-tech pseudo-solutions to fight male violence against women or will your party support feminist advocacy and support services?

14

Housing Policy

Pam Sayne, Jane Robinson and GROOTS
with Jennifer Chew

In 1992, the federal Conservatives cancelled all social housing programs, resulting in deteriorating housing for low and moderate income Canadians. There has been no new federal funding for low income housing units since 1993. In 1996, the Liberal government proposed a complete withdrawal from social housing by transferring the administration of this sector to the provinces.

Canadian households must spend increasing amounts of their fixed or declining incomes on rent. This is disproportionately experienced by women-led households, which have, on average, half the income of male-led households. Immigrants, refugees, urban Aboriginal peoples, elderly women, single mothers, and people with disabilities in particular, experience an increase in housing costs and a decrease in housing options. Homelessness has increased in all Canadian cities.

Liberal Record

The direction of the Liberal government has continued the decline initiated by the Tories. The 1993 Liberal Red Book of election promises contained no commitments to housing, and the Chrétien government has few achievements on record regarding the provision of secure and affordable social housing to low and moderate income Canadians. (Some funds were diverted from social housing to emergency shelters, and over a two-year period $100 million was reinstated to the Homeowner and Disabled components of the Residential Rehabilitation Assistance Program.) In some provinces, public housing is being sold off to the private sector, and this is threatened to happen in others. The once-prominent Canada Mortgage and Housing Corporation has been reduced to underwriting mortgages, funding research, maintaining a Native-on-Reserve housing program and promoting Canadian housing products internationally. CMHC will be further weakened by massive staff layoffs in 1997.

The Liberal housing policy emphasizes cutbacks and transferring of responsibilities to the provinces. In the proposed revisions to the National Housing Act, the Liberals claim to uphold the principle of providing housing for people of the lowest income. However, since 1993 the record shows a continued dismantling of social housing and an alarming trend towards privatization.

In June 1996, the government of Canada signed the Habitat Agenda at the United Nations World Conference on Human Settlements in Istanbul, Turkey. Commitments made in this Agenda include the provision of adequate shelter for all, the "need to improve and ensure access by those belonging to vulnerable and disadvantaged groups to shelter, finance, infrastructure, basic social services, safety nets and decision-making processes within national and international enabling environments," and the assurance that government would continue to address women's housing needs in all phases of the development and management of housing, including appropriate community development strategies.

Based on this background and these commitments, a list of questions was sent to all federal parties in November 1996. No responses were received. This is a clear indication that women's groups must be vigilant about the issue of housing. To this end, we are suggesting that the following questions be used when meeting and lobbying candidates and politicians.

Questions:

1. What would your party do to reduce the homelessness that is affecting the citizens of Canada, in particular, women?

2. Canada is a signatory to the Habitat Agenda that guarantees adequate housing for all. How would your party and the CMHC work together to honour this commitment?

3. Would your party stop the devolution of co-op, non-profit and public housing responsibilities to the provinces and impose measures to prohibit the privatization of public housing?

4. How will you stop the provinces from abdicating their social housing responsibility? How would you see the federal government bringing together the private, non-profit and municipal sectors to assist in the provision of affordable housing?

15

Women's International Solidarity and Foreign Policy

The International Solidarity Committee

Relationships between countries and among countries are governed by international laws in such areas as human rights, justice and labour, and by bilateral or multilateral agreements on economic issues, trade and immigration. These laws and agreements do not have a neutral effect on women and children. For example, women bear the brunt of "Structural Adjustment Programs" (SAPs).

What is a SAP? Before any country's government can borrow money from international financial institutions (mostly used for debt payments), the World Bank and the International Monetary Fund (IMF) review the country's financial plan to make sure the country's government abides by their conditions. These conditions make up the package of SAPs. They require, among other things: cuts in social spending, a fixation on deficit reduction, privatization of public services and programs, and state deregulation. The World Bank and the IMF, controlled by the wealthy G-7 countries, then make recommendations to the lending institutions. A favourable recommendation depends on whether and how a country's government would implement the SAPs according to the specified conditions. Individual countries are essentially held hostage to external demands on how to control their domestic affairs. The World Bank and the IMF look very unfavourably at, for example, food subsidies for urban residents.

Most governments implement SAPs and trade agreements to the detriment of people's lives, their livelihood and their environment and to the benefit of corporations wishing to do business in the affected countries. The implementation of SAPs leads to increased unemployment, dismantling of social programs, erosion of democratic structures, the violation of human rights and environmental degradation in both industrialized and developing countries. As a result, the inequalities based on gender, race and class become more severe. SAPs, then, can be rightfully called a re-colonization process that is in the hands of those who control the World Bank and the IMF.

International agreements on so-called "free" trade also come with a hefty price for women and children. Agreements such as the North American Free Trade Agreement (NAFTA) between Canada, the US and Mexico require that governments eliminate business "barriers" so government and private institutions can freely compete across the borders. Demands made by corporations — and formalized in these agreements — include the elimination of subsidies to local producers, environmental policies that prohibit wastes and pollution, labour standards that protect workers from contracting out and privatization, and so on. If a corporation finds that its profits are lower due to government regulations, higher wages and other labour benefits, it is free to move its business to countries where higher profits can be attained, where labour is cheaper and where government regulations are less restrictive. This is the only "free" thing about free trade.

The effects of SAPs and unfair free trade on the lives of women and children are dramatic. Working women are forced to accept much cheaper value for their labour, less benefits and worsening working conditions. Most often, there are no jobs. Many women, especially from the developing countries, are forced to leave their children, families and relatives and migrate to other countries where their labour is in demand, often for domestic work.

As migrant workers, women are vulnerable to different forms of exploitation and abuse, such as low wages, long working hours, very few or no benefits, lack of privacy, emotional, physical or sexual harassment, and so on. Most of these women experience violence. In the past few years there have even been cases where women have been threatened with the death penalty for defending themselves against abusive employers.

What is unfair and unjust is that these women make valuable contributions both in their own countries and in the countries where they currently work, contributions that have consistently been undermined and undervalued by those who profit by them.

The global profit-driven economic model has deepened the economic crisis and impoverished women. Structural Adjustment Programs and free trade agreements have increased the power of transnational corporations and have placed corporations practically beyond accountability of governments and peoples. Ironically, this unprecedented power has come about with the substantial aid of elites within the governments of these different countries. For example, in Canada, the Liberal government has recently laid the groundwork for further liberalization of world trade by adopting the recommendations of the ministerial meeting of the World Trade Organization held in Singapore. In this latest international agreement, the protection of labour standards was left off the table!

Liberal's Pre-Election Promises
While in opposition, the Liberals' foreign policy handbook promised to create an independent foreign policy think tank. The Liberals also promised to publish annual reports on the human rights records of other governments before granting them aid. The Liberals also advocated a curb on arms exports

and denounced US cruise-missile testing across Canadian territory.

Questions:

1. Canada has not become a signatory of the 1990 United Nations Convention on the Protection of the Rights of All Migrant Workers and Members of their Families. This Convention was adopted by the UN General Assembly Resolution 45/158 on December 18, 1990, but to be enforced it must be signed and ratified by 20 UN member countries. What is your party's position in regards to Canada becoming a signatory of this convention?

Liberal Party (Liberals)
The Liberals have stated that they will not sign this Convention.

Bloc Québécois (Bloc)
The Bloc are in favour of signing this Convention.
However, they state that it is up to the provincial governments to decide on this issue.

Reform Party (Reform)
Reform state that each UN Convention must be evaluated on its own merits but did not answer the question in regards to this particular UN Convention.

New Democratic Party (NDP)
The NDP are in favour of Canada becoming a signatory to this Convention.

Progressive Conservative Party
Failed to respond.

2. Would your party link Canada's trade and foreign policy to a country's internationally recognized record on human

rights, so that neither the Canadian government nor Canadian companies could give foreign aid to or trade with a country that practices human rights violations?

Liberal Party (Liberals)

The Liberal Party has not linked a country's human rights record to Canada's trade or foreign policy. Instead, the Liberals have consistently ignored the demands of human rights activists and continue to trade (and encourage even greater trade) with human rights abusers.

Bloc Québécois

Failed to respond.

Reform Party (Reform)

Reform state that they do not support giving foreign aid to governments that suppress "basic" human rights. They are silent, however, on the issue of trade with human rights violators.

Reform would, however, reduce foreign aid.

New Democratic Party

Failed to respond.

Progressive Conservative Party (Tories)

The Tories say that "concern for the human rights records of our trading partners must continue to form a critical part of Canada's trade policy."

But they add that, along with human rights advocacy, the "monitoring" of population growth would also be key to a Tory government's foreign and trade policy.

Additionally, they also state that "expanding secured access to international markets for Canadian goods and services remains *the first priority* of Canadian international trade policy" (emphasis added).

3. Would your party initiate proposals to replace SAPs with more equitable and socially oriented policies and programs that complement an individual country's long-term development objectives?

Liberal Party (Liberals)

The Liberals have not stated that they would do so. They state only that "the government must work to eliminate conditions attached to loans, aid and structural adjustment programs which increase women's poverty and undermine their economic security." They add that "the government can do this through its own programs, such as the Official Development Assistance, and through its influence in international bodies such as the G-7, the International Monetary Fund, the World Bank and other multilateral institutions." However, they do not state whether they will do so or not.

Bloc Québécois

Failed to respond.

Reform Party

Failed to respond.

New Democratic Party (NDP)

The NDP state they "support debt relief of countries whose international debt burden overwhelms their economic capacity to supply basic human needs. Debt relief must be a component of any international strategy to assist the most hard-pressed nations, especially those in sub-Saharan Africa with few prospects for earning foreign currencies through exports."

The NDP would insist that Canada's investment in international and regional development banks be accounted for through Parliament and that the funds channelled through these banks be used for sustainable projects more directly related to meeting basic needs. The environmental impact of projects should be assessed and projects should complement the long-term development objectives of individual countries.

Progressive Conservative Party (Tories)
> The Tories *support traditional Structural Adjustment Programs.* They state that "official development assistance must encourage countries to become and remain self-sufficient, and open the door for trade and economic development for both Canada and the recipient country."

4. Would ending poverty and achieving women's equality in the country and internationally be central to your government's foreign policy? Would you resume and increase foreign aid based on this perspective, instead of based on market-driven considerations?

Liberal Party (Liberals)
> The Liberals' record shows that they have not considered the achievement of women's equality or the eradication of poverty as central to the formation or implementation of foreign and trade policies.

Bloc Québécois (Bloc)
> The Bloc "subscribe" to the observations contained in the report of the Special Joint Committee that is examining Canada's foreign policy.
>
> The report states that improvements in achieving the equal status of women in society are fundamental aspects of sustainable development. To this end, education for girls, reproductive health services, reform of legal systems and the strengthening of women's organizations, among others, must be targetted. Moreover, women must be involved in all sector-based programs as decision-makers, partici-

pants and beneficiaries of development. The report points out that improvements to women's status bring great benefits to society.

Reform Party (Reform)

The Reform Party has not considered the achievement of women's equality or the eradication of poverty when forming or implementing its foreign and trade policies.

A Reform government expects savings from a reduction in spending and possible merger and refocusing of the Foreign Affairs and International Trade department.

Reform would significantly reduce the Canadian International Development Agency (CIDA).

New Democratic Party (NDP)

The NDP state that "ending poverty and achieving women's equality are central to their approach to foreign policy."

They would increase both the quantity and quality of their development assistance, setting a longterm goal of bringing spending on development assistance roughly in balance with their military spending — about 15 percent of the GNP for both.

The NDP would strive "to reduce the commercialization of Canada's development programs and ensure that dollars spent are aimed at the poorest countries and that the goal of women's equality is central to all decision about aid."

Progressive Conservative Party (Tories)

The Tories have not considered the achievement of women's equality or the eradication of poverty when forming or implementing its foreign and trade policies.

They state that "priority for non-emergency aid will be given to those countries that are willing to work with Canada's value system and to projects which encourage self-sufficiency and economic growth."

The following questions did not receive sufficient responses from enough of the federal parties for NAC to be able to present a comparison of their views on these issues. However, you are encouraged to ask these questions of those seeking your vote.

5. Would your party give women, especially marginalized women (Aboriginal women, women of colour, women with disabilities, women in poverty, lesbians) access to the decision-making processes in international treaties, agreements and conferences?

6. Would your party ensure that the Asia Pacific Economic Cooperation (APEC), another form of trade agreement in the Asia Pacific region, comply with the international norms and standards set forth under the Convention on the Elimination of All Forms of Discrimination Against Women?

7. Would your party initiate proposals to APEC member countries that set economic and trade priorities based on social infrastructure and equity principles that benefit the common good rather than corporate profits?

8. Would your party commit financial and other resources to establish policies and mechanisms to implement, in Canada, the UN Platform for Action, which works toward the achievement of women's equality, agreed upon by member countries of the United Nations at the Fourth World Conference on Women in Beijing in September 1995?

9. Would your party initiate proposals to the World Bank and International Monetary Fund that would cancel the debts of developing countries in order to alleviate the suffering of these countries, which spend more per capita on debt servicing than on basic human needs and rights?

Appendix I

Funding for Women's Organizations and Feminist Research

In 1973, the Women's Program was created as part of the Secretary of State to provide support for women's organizations working towards women's equality. In 1997, two types of funding are provided under Status of Women Canada: project funding (mostly under $15,000 per project) and program funding (commonly known as "core" funding), which supports the organizational infrastructure of equality seeking women's groups, such as women's centers.

New organizations have not received "core" funding since 1989 because of "budget constraints." This has meant that new groups, in particular groups of Aboriginal women, women with disabilities, women of colour and women in rural areas, have not had access to needed resources to adequately carry out their work.

In 1990, the Conservative government attempted to completely cut "core" funding to all the women's centres as well as to other women's organizations they were funding (for example, women's publications). When women in Newfoundland occupied the offices of the Secretary of State responsible for the Status of Women and other women began to do the same in their areas, the government backed down on the cuts to women's centres. However, the funding these groups still receive has been cut by a minimum of 25 percent since 1990.

In 1996, the Canadian Advisory Council on the Status of Women, a semi-independent group first created in 1973 and which funded research and advised the government on women's issues, was also eliminated. In 1997, Status of Women Canada conducted a consultation with women's groups across the country. Recommendations were made about the Women's Program and also about the newly created research arm of the Status of Women, the Independent Policy Research Fund, designed to replace the Canadian Advisory Committee on the Status of Women.

Women said that the Policy Research Fund

• should be independent, and

• that grassroots/activist women should be involved in selecting research projects.

Women's groups are concerned about what role grassroots women will actually be able to play and if they will be able to access any research funding.

In the consultation, women had some strong messages about the Women's Program. They said that

• the current funding is not sufficient to meet the Program's mandate and that additional funding is required, and

• "core" funding for organizations is essential, and this funding should also be extended to more recently emerging equality seeking women's groups.

In response, Status of Women say that they cannot provide the funding needed by women's organizations. They have instead committed themselves to attempting to "gain access to additional resources" from other agencies and departments and to helping women's groups with fundraising strategies.

The Status of Women are also proposing, in order to create "greater flexibility," a change in "funding mecha-

nisms to be able to respond to changing community needs
and issues." They appear to be moving further and further
away from "core" funding and towards a "project" type of
funding. They are already requiring organizations to carry
out a "specific program of activities, with clearly defined,
concrete outcomes that address the objectives." Status of
Women staff are telling organizations that they are no longer
funding organizational infrastructures.

Women's groups fear that "greater flexibility" and a move
away from "core funding" will mean that more groups will
be increasingly competing with one another for a shrinking
pot of money. Women's groups worry they may be facing
greater insecurity and instability.

The total operating budget of Status of Women Canada in
1996/97 was less than $8 million. This translates into slightly
more than $.50 per year per woman or girl in the country.
The Women's Program funding for women's groups and for
supporting offices in all the regions of the country was less
than $2.5 million. Surely we deserve more than this. Women
do pay taxes. Ultimately, this is our money and more of it
should be dedicated to working for equality.

Status of Women stress to groups that they must have
projects with measurable outcomes so there is accountability
for the funding. Staff talk about educating groups about the
expectations of the Women's Program. Status of Women,
however, need to realize that women in Canada have expectations of them, that they are accountable to us. It is our
money they are spending. Our recommendations must be
their priorities.

Questions:

1. Does your party support an increase in the Women's
Program budget?
   2. Is your party committed to ensuring "core" funding for
women's groups?

Women's Guide to All Candidates' Meetings

There are a number of ways in which women can be heard in our political system. This information is not something that is promoted by governments and politicians. Some of us are familiar with letter-writing campaigns, marches, demonstrations, and so on. Many of us are unaware that we have the power to organize and call All Candidates' Meetings. This type of meeting is a crucial way to hold our MPs accountable, to elicit their views on various issues and to secure their commitment to action.

Your MP can be heavily influenced through strategic organizing in your electoral riding. Women have the power to make an impact, but it is something that we need to take better advantage of. A group of five women making a meeting place and a request to your MP and the Opposition Party members in your riding to attend is all it takes to organize a meeting!

It is a good idea to work with a women's organization or community-based organization in this undertaking. In this way you can take advantage of the resources in your community and elicit some support in informing other members of the community about the meeting so that they have the opportunity to participate.

It is important to have your questions prepared so that your issues will be addressed. Due to the popularity of All Candidates' Meetings, chances are someone has already planned one during an election campaign. It is important to go to these meetings. Women's issues will not be heard or acted upon unless we demand accountability from our elected officials.

It is also a good idea to organize like-minded women and allies in your community to share information and start an education process about the impact of government policies and practices on women's lives. We hope that *The National Action Committee on the Status of Women's Voters' Guide: A Women's Agenda for Social Justice* aids you in this important and meaningful work.

Appendix III

How to Get Involved in NAC

The National Action Committee on the Status of women (NAC) is the largest feminist organization in Canada. NAC is made up of a coalition of over 650 member groups and in 1997 we are celebrating our twenty-fifth anniversary of fighting for women's equality. NAC's membership is diverse and broad-based. We are women's centres, women's organizations fighting male violence against women, trade unions, Aboriginal and Métis women's groups, women immigrants and refugees organizations, lesbian organizations, women of colour, student groups, women with disabilities, business women's groups and much, much more.

NAC recently organized, with the Canadian Labour Congress, the most successful grassroots action ever taken by women in Canadian history. Women from all parts of the country and all walks of life participated in the National Women's March Against Poverty: For Bread and Roses and in Jobs and Justice during May and June of 1996. The Quebec Women's March for Bread and Roses in 1995 served as the inspiration for this historic action in Canada. Over 100,000 women from coast to coast participated. The 15 demands of the March have not all been met by the government and they remain integral to NAC's priority work.

NAC's Executive Committee is made up of 27 volunteer members who are elected by our membership in elections held regionally and at our Annual General Meeting. NAC is supported by a handful of paid staff and by volunteer committees. Through an ever-growing, diverse membership,

NAC is able to organize at a grassroots level. We are involved in demonstrations, popular education work, direct action, letter-writing campaigns and lobbying of federal, provincial and territorial governments. We are engaged in international solidarity work, conference organizing, research and special events planning.

NAC currently receives 75 percent of its funding from membership fees, individuals and group donors and from other fundraising activities across the country. At one time we were 100 percent funded by the federal government. Through an ongoing process of regionalization — strengthening of our 14 regions — we are becoming more and more able to organize at the local level.

We have a national office that is located in Toronto, Ontario, and our Regional Representatives are located in each province and territory. To become more involved, the first step is to get in touch with the Regional Representative in your province or territory. We have many issues committees through which national, regional and local networks of women are able to do the work that is relevant to their lives and area of interest. To find out who your Regional Representative is, call the national office of NAC and we will gladly put you in touch with her.